The Biblical Seminar
54

A MANUAL OF
HERMENEUTICS

A MANUAL OF HERMENEUTICS

Luis Alonso Schökel
with José María Bravo

Translated by Liliana M. Rosa
Further editing by Brook W.R. Pearson

Sheffield Academic Press

Copyright © 1998 Sheffield Academic Press

Published by
Sheffield Academic Press Ltd
Mansion House
19 Kingfield Road
Sheffield S11 9AS
England

Typeset by Sheffield Academic Press
and
Printed on acid-free paper in Great Britain
by The Cromwell Press

British Library Cataloguing in Publication Data

A catalogue record for this book is available
from the British Library

ISBN 1-85075-850-6

CONTENTS

Part II

TEXT-HERMENEUTICS

PREFACE

A manual is a work that can be done at the beginning or the end of a teaching career. Inexperienced teachers opening their way through the material, daunted and solicitous in front of their pupils, write a manual for mutual help. It clarifies their ideas because they have to express them, and makes the work of comprehension easier for their pupils. Such a manual is provisional, probably brief and can be developed.

If the manual is composed at the end of a career, after years of explaining the subject and with retirement in sight, this manual can also be brief. This is because, this time, the theme has matured with reflection, and the formulas have become clearly defined through repetition. At that moment, the teachers can allow themselves the difficult brevity of what has been distilled or decanted. Their aspiration is to offer density without obscurity, order without exhibition.

In the final stage of composing this work, the collaboration of two pupils has accompanied me. Jeremías Lera wrote class notes in my penultimate year of teaching (using materials I gave him, together with my oral explanations in class). When I stepped over the threshold of retirement, José María Bravo, who had graduated in Scripture, sacrificed two Christmas holidays and, in discussion with Lera and using his notes, prepared the final edition. We both wish to thank the Centro Español de Estudios Eclesiásticos (the Spanish Centre of Ecclesiastical Studies) and its rector, Monsignor Justo Fernández Alonso, for the assignment of a grant for the completion of this book.

If we keep the title of 'manual', it is not to detract from its value, but rather to denote modestly its function, whose reward is its usefulness.

Luis Alonso Schökel
Rome, Christmas 1992

STARTING ON THE SUBJECT

The generic theme of this manual is hermeneutics. This specific theme limits it to literary texts. Some sections and many examples come from the biblical field. Specificity is of central importance. Leaving aside juridical texts, research studies and purely didactic writings, whose rules are to some extent different, I concentrate on literary texts in the wider sense.

Naturally, when explaining what is specific, many generic concepts have to be used, applicable in part to texts that are not literary. The simple term 'hermeneutics' can thus be justified as the title of the book. However, in many cultures, religious texts hold a privileged position among literary texts (myths, legends, tales, prayers). Religious literature is prior to theology. Some of these texts of religious literature may appear to have special attributes, either because they are ascribed a supernatural origin, or because they are subjected to normative interpretation: the Enuma Elish, the epic of Gilgamesh, Pop Vuh, the Bible, the Koran. For that reason (bearing in mind my personal activity in the sphere), to the central block devoted to literary texts I have thought it fit to add a number of considerations on the supernatural origin of the Bible and its normative interpretation, as understood by Christians. In these sections, I move from what is specific to what is individual.

For that reason, the first essay on inspiration should not lead to confusion. Its object is to explain the religious text and its explication in terms of the reality of language and literary work. There is a parallelism and continuity between the shift in the theory of inspiration and the shift in hermeneutical theory.

The abundance of biblical examples should not cause surprise. It is the result of my long years of activity and of shared convictions. I feel easily at home in the Bible, and many people consider the Bible to be the most important book in universal literature. It is an exceptional literary text.

Philip ran up to him, heard that he was reading the prophecy of Isaiah, and asked him, 'Do you understand what you are reading?'

He answered: 'And how can I understand it if no one explains it to me?' (Acts 8.30-31).

A man reads as he goes along. He understands the words, he knows the system of signs that follow one after another in his reading, he grasps the coherence of the text, but it eludes him, and he does not really understand what he is reading. He needs a guide, an interpreter— someone or something that will help him to understand.

When readers do not understand the meaning of a text, comprehension must be facilitated with an explanation. We often face a similar situation when dealing with literary texts, especially when they belong to another period or culture; which is why commentaries have always been and continue to be necessary in order to lead to comprehension. Here I am not going to explain texts, but rather reflect on the activities of interpreting and understanding.

Chapter 1

INTRODUCTION

1. *Clarification of Terms*

From the outset, it is useful to have a clear triple distinction within the task of interpreting literary texts. I make this distinction in order to give hermeneutics its appropriate position, defined relative to other levels of interpretation, comprehension and explanation of literary texts.

(1)   Exegesis: the exercise of comprehending and interpreting a text.
(2)   The exegetical method: the way of proceeding systematically in the interpretation of a text.
(3)   Hermeneutics: the theory of the activity of understanding and interpreting texts.

It is as if we were in a building on different levels. A complex and differentiated activity is developed on the first level, which, in turn, is criss-crossed by multiple relationships and contacts. We call such activity 'exegesis'. From a little higher up, a different vision is obtained of what happens below; it becomes possible to explain organically the activity developed. Looking down from the second level we discover design and purpose, aim and means; from this vantage point, we may describe the method of exegetical activity. There is still a third and higher plane with a position that offers an ample overall survey of the whole building. It is the place where essential principles may be uncovered and stated. This is the level of hermeneutical reflection.

Let us take the example of the Sunday sermon. It consists of the interpretation of biblical texts which have just been read. The texts form part of a liturgical context which interprets them, and at the same time are translations (interpretations) of the original texts. The translations and commentary are based on the technical interpretation (exegesis) of experts. Besides this, a series of interpretations is accumulated on the text in the form of tradition. And again, the text of the New Testament has interpreted the text of the Old Testament, which, in turn, incorporates interpretations. There will probably also have been the singing of a biblical text: the music interprets the words and is interpreted by both the choir and the congregation.

Standards, rules and guidelines can be established for these steps: they may be organized and articulated in a coherent method, to better and more surely find and expound the sense of the texts.

There are many methods in literary research, which I will investigate, each with its own standards and procedures, focusing on specific elements in the text: sources, traditions, literary genres, redaction, influences and similarities, among others. After all this I will be able to distance myself from my own interpretative method.

I am able to achieve this distance by organizing the method, by controlling its application, and by explicating others' attempts at the same process. I distance myself from my interpretative method and its application, setting them as a problem to be investigated. It is a complex problem because it includes several aspects: psychological (by which mental activity do I understand the text?); ontological (about the conditions of possibility); scientific (how far the method I use is legitimate, if it is accurate or not, if it excludes arbitrariness); sociological (how my education affects my way of interpreting, my culture, my environment, my position and my activity in society); existential (how I interpret myself confronting the text); phenomenological (what a text is, how it exists, how a text is produced); theological (how to interpret a text which is a communication from God); biblical (peculiarities offered by a literary text that is so specific).

a. *Hermeneutics Is Neither Exegesis, Nor a Type of Exegesis*
Exegesis is an approach to the text in order to explain its meaning. We need to understand what the words actually mean, how the different statements are grouped, and how they are constructed and organized. For this we may use criteria based on the nature and devices of a literary language (study of the literary forms, rhetorical tropes and figures, structural and stylistic analysis).

For example, in Mt. 19.30 we read, 'But many who are first will be last, and the last first'. Then follows the parable of the labourers in the vineyard, which ends in 20.16: 'So the last will be first, and the first last'. In many editions of the New Testament, 19.30 seems to have no relation with the parable in question, but rather with the text that precedes it. However, on carrying out a stylistic analysis, we recognize here the use of an inclusion—a stylistic formula used to frame a narrative period, in such a way that it begins and ends with the same idea or phrase. This is why, in order to understand the parable correctly, it is necessary to take it from 19.30, and not begin with the following verse, as is suggested from the division made by the subtitles which are added to many editions of the New Testament.

In exegetical work, we are usually interested in a series of factors that directly or indirectly affect the text. (E.g. it may be necessary to know something about the author, his or her culture and psychology, his or her social and historical situation.) When we have reached this level of knowledge of data related to the text, we may affirm that we feel capable of understanding its sense and of explaining it, but we have to recognise that all we have done is carried out a methodical, organised, systematic piece of work about a literary text—we may not identify this process with hermeneutics, the theory of comprehension and textual interpretation.

From reflection on the findings of existentialist philosophy, as well as from the study of human communication, new values of texts have been stressed: besides autonomy and information, the text's capacity to appeal and stir readers by its message has been emphasized. A vital current is produced, a current that urges readers to interpret the text along an existentialist line, in the sense of asking themselves what the text tells them, what personal actualization this demanding message may elicit. This is what we call *actualized comprehension* of the text, a different type of exegesis. Yet it should not be called hermeneutical interpretation (as some incorrectly do).

The reading of a text is an act that transfers us to the reality which gave rise to the writing. When the sense of a written communication is grasped, not only are sentences read, but also the ideas and truths that are expressed in the text can be acquired and known.

Through the activity of interpretation we become aware of the necessity to span a distance, the necessity to become adapted as readers to a text that proves to be difficult, alien to us; exegesis is basically explanation. However, hermeneutics is not an alternative to exegesis. Exegesis is the explanation of a text according to its original meaning—historical-critical work. Existentialist exegesis is the explanation of the text according to the meaning it has for readers. They are two ways of carrying out exegesis, of explaining the text, but they are clearly not hermeneutics.

b. *Hermeneutics Is Not about Exegetical Method*

A method is a systematic way of doing something. 'Method' is the term applied to a set of rules or exercises used to learn something.[1] A method is a definite and controlled way of proceeding. It is not the fact of doing something, but rather the way in which it is done.

I have already pointed out that many methods may be used for the study of the Bible. For example, studying the story of Jesus' infancy, we apply a method which fundamentally makes use of the analysis of literary genres; thus, these texts are interpreted as haggadic midrash, and within them we discover periods schematized under the literary form of a genealogical list, other sections elaborated with the model of accounts of annunciation, hymns of praise, and so on. It is an interpretative orientation defined by the use of a previously defined method.

Let us take the case of Lk. 10.25-37: a dialogue, in the middle of which the parable of the Good Samaritan is inserted. It is a well constructed narrative, with characters that come on the scene and leave it, with different scenarios, a riveting crescendo. And at the end, a command: 'Go, and do as he did.' Readers at the end of the twentieth century also listen to this order, and ask themselves, 'What must I do? How can I be a good Samaritan in this day and age? How can I cure the injured I find in my way? In short, how can I live the message of this story in my person today, here and now?'

This type of comprehending and interpreting the text by asking pertinent questions is valid and useful, but, nevertheless, this still remains simply in the realm of exegetical method. It is possible to define which rules, steps and actions are valid and appropiate in order to understand and interpret texts, but the method elaborated is still not valid theoretical reflection on the act of understanding and interpreting texts; it is not hermeneutics.

Summary. Hermeneutics is the theory of the comprehension and interpretation of literary texts. It differs from the exegetical method (the systematic way of proceeding in comprehension) and from exegesis (the exercise of comprehension and interpretation).

---

1.   Maria Moliner, *Diccionario del uso del español* (Madrid: Gredos, 1966).

2. *Types of Interpretation*

In his *Teoria generale della interpretazione*[2] Emilio Betti gives a classification of types of interpretation of literary texts according to their respective functions. He distinguishes three basic types of interpretation: reproductive, explicative and normative.

(1) *Reproductive* interpretation consists in 'performing' the text. For example, a poet when he or she recites a poem, the performance of a play, the performance of a piece of music, the personal reading of a text: all these are actions that reproduce the work or make it present.

The example of the theatre reflects this type of performance very well. The actor plays the part of a character; on the stage he or she does not carry out an irrelevant action, but plays the role, bringing to life the character represented; the written work thus recovers its authentic existence on the stage. The actor's performance reproduces the character and brings it to life as he or she personifies it.

(2) *Explicative* interpretation supposes that we intend to attain a reproductive interpretation, which is the important one, since it makes the text present and gives it life.

Listeners or readers sometimes do not grasp the meaning in the communication of a message, which is why explicative interpretation is necessary; it tries to mediate, making the meaning accessible. If I listen to the aria 'Recitar' from the opera *I pagliacci*, I grasp a melody and words filled with intense drama, the expression of profound feelings, sadness and fury that arise together. Shortly afterwards I find the libretto of the opera, I read the words of the aria; and thanks to a musical critic, I know the situation of the character: a clown who has to play his part in the circus in the midst of an intimate personal situation of sorrow for betrayed love. When I listen to the aria again, I enjoy it even more. The same will happen after a critical analysis of the musical score.

The example of language interpreters may also be of use to us. They are the mediators of meaning between two people who do not share the same language. Their task is to help them to understand, and while they carry out simultaneous translation, they are favouring the reproduction of the message by means of the work of mediation-explanation.

2. E. Betti, *Teoria generale della interpretazione* (Milan: Dott. A. Giuffrè, 1955), pp. 343-49.

(3) The *normative* function still lies within the sphere of the meaning of the text. It is the function that defines the meaning of a given text with authority, which may be normative in terms of either understanding, or of action.

Let us take the example of Jn 14.28: 'If you loved me, you would be glad that I am going to the Father, for the Father is greater than I am.' This verse was used by the Arians as their argument in the christological disputes of the fourth century; with it they wanted to defend their stand that the Son could be understood only as a creature of the Father's will. However, the Church with its authority defined that the text cannot be understood in terms of an ontological inferiority of the Son with respect to the Father. This is a normative interpretation, binding for those who believe.

Our primary interest is in the first two functions, which help us to understand what I have said up to here. In interpretation, it is necessary to differentiate the philological, technical and critical moments from the reproduction or representation of the text. But there is yet a further dimension.

3. *Hermeneutics: The Theory of Comprehension–Interpretation*

Does Beethoven's fifth symphony exist? Yes, we have often listened to it. However, it is a fact that we have been able to listen to different interpretations of this score. Music exists only when the score is played—the score is no more than a register, a form of conserving the written message by means of a series of conventional signs. First, the interpreter has to master the signs, to know what each one represents—tone, duration, intensity, in what key and tonality the work is written. Once the signs are understood, they may be performed: it is then that the music exists anew, when the work registered in the score comes to life.

Suppose we take one of Quevedo's sonnets, or a Lope de Vega drama. We even know some texts by heart, and it is enough for us to hear a familiar phrase to be able to recite a fragment of a play. We are capable of reciting a poem, we enjoy a play. The world, events, circumstances, characters and feelings that writers like Quevedo or Lope de Vega recorded in their works do not remain cloistered away in their written notations, but, thanks to them, are within our reach, and come to life every time they are recited or put on the stage.

However, let us return to our question: Does Beethoven's fifth symphony exist? What is it? What does a symphony consist of? How can it be elucidated? If it belongs to the world of music, what is music? What use is it? How is music made? Let us consider Psalm 122, one of the songs interpreted by the Jewish people on pilgrimage to Jerusalem to celebrate their feast days. For us, this psalm is recorded in a particular textual body of prayers called the book of Psalms. It belongs to a characteristic group of psalms, those intoned on pilgrimage or songs on the way up to Jerusalem. It has a specific literary form, its own rhythm; it uses precise terms. Nevertheless, what is a psalm? What is a religious poem? What does this particular text say? What does it require of me? How can I make it mine?

These questions may be asked in the face of all written communication, of any literary text. How does a text arise? How does it reach me? What does it tell me? How is the message it transmits conditioned by the language? What presuppositions do I possess as a reader? What conditioning factors lie in me? This is the field of general hermeneutics, of the theorizing on the comprehension and interpretation of literary texts.

Summary. According to their function, the types of interpretation of texts are: reproductive, explicative and normative. Hermeneutics is the theoretical reflection on the understanding and interpretation of texts.

Part I

INSPIRATION, LANGUAGE AND HERMENEUTICS

INTRODUCTION

The theories of hermeneutics have a relationship of correlativity with those of biblical inspiration. These two theories condition each other. Within my hermeneutical proposition, biblical hermeneutics plays an important part—it should not be forgotten that the interpretation of biblical texts has been the sphere where most hermeneutical activity and reflection have developed over time. That is why I am going to begin by putting forward some ideas on the theme of inspiration, which will give way to the development of my hermeneutical reflection.

A fundamental characteristic that we find in the Bible is that the sacred writers proffer a communication claiming to be a word, a message from God. Jews and Christians believe that these authors were inspired or assisted in a special way by a divine gift, since the message they transmit belongs, in the first place, to the sphere of God, who wants to communicate with us. The hermeneutical orientation one takes with regard to the Bible will depend a great deal on what one understands by 'inspiration'; in the same way, one's concept of inspiration will substantially mark one's hermeneutical orientation.

Chapter 2

INSPIRATION FROM THE PERSPECTIVE OF JUDGMENT
AND FROM THE PERSPECTIVE OF LANGUAGE

St Thomas Aquinas taught us to place prophecy (not strictly inspiration) in the context of the *charismata* or of the *gratiae gratis datae*
(*Summa Theol.* 171-78). He divides the charismata into three groups:

(1)   the grace of knowing (*charisma cognoscendi*)
(2)   the grace of speaking (*charisma loquendi*)
(3)   the grace of acting (*charisma agendi*).

Using this division he situated the *charisma* of prophecy in the first
group, and so it is understood as the *charisma* of knowledge. This is the
presupposition on which is later developed the treatise *De Inspiratione
Sacrae Scripturae*, which consequently understands inspiration as a
question of knowledge. Let us see how inspiration is conceived according to this perspective.

1. Inspiration from the Perspective of Judgment

By judgment, we mean *intellectual* judgment, the mental act that
affirms or denies something. Perception, statement and reasoning may
be distinguished in the world of mental knowledge. The biblical author
may receive knowledge directly from God, by previous revelation. This
revelation may come by different ways: vision, imagination, intellectual perception, among others.

However, on numerous occasions, the prophets obtain information in
human terms: by their own efforts, by their own experience, by their
observation of the reality that surrounds them, by contact with other
people. The writers must ponder over whether what they have been told
or what they have known is true or not. It is at this moment in the
process of human learning that God acts, when the authors develop a

logical judgment. It is at that instant when God inspires them so that the prophets see things by the light of divine truth, by God's light. On producing the statement that follows this perception, a divine intervention is produced, thus guaranteeing the truth of the judgment emitted after the sacred writers' perceptions. Following on this judgment comes the decision to communicate it, but it is God who moves human will to write, without taking liberty away; under the infallible action of God, human decision is in a way divine: God is the author of the process, and so too of the book.

a. *Responses*

A possible series of consequences arises immediately from such a conception of inspiration. One possible response is an obsessive preoccupation with biblical infallibility: every statement in the Scripture must be true, nothing can hold any error. As the Bible is an inspired text, the enunciations it contains cannot be false because they come from God. Another possible response is that of fundamentalism, which defends the truth of every biblical phrase exactly as it stands and sounds, going so far that the Bible is fragmented into an infinity of infallible enunciations.

At the other end of the spectrum, the Bible acquires an absolute, ahistorical character. Judgment is something absolute and unconditioned, no matter when it was pronounced; it has nothing to do with history.

Finally, there follows a disinterest for literary forms, and even forms of language. In this position, since the only thing of importance is the truth of the enunciation, how it is formulated is of no concern.

b. *Practical Judgment*

By way of example, recourse can be made to the sapiential books, for example, Prov. 26.14: 'A door turns on its hinges, a sluggard, on his bed'; people repeat this adage and the inspired author takes it and writes it down. When the author does this, and in so doing, canonizes it, he or she acts under God's light. But where would intellectual judgment lie in the Psalms or in the Song of Songs? In order to solve these problems something must be added: together with theoretical judgment, scholars introduced the concept of practical judgment. This has as its objective not the *truth* of the enunciation, but rather the *appropriateness* of the formulation. The author judges that he or she must write precisely those words, in exactly that way.

This addition of practical judgment differentiates and perfects the previous schema. It means progress, insofar as it draws nearer to the psychological reality of literary creation; yet everything still remains focused on judgment. Thus the theory stands, while at the same time giving a little explanation of what does not work.

2. *Inspiration from the Perspective of Language*

I prefer to adopt a radically different position, to shift the place of the theory of inspiration and contemplate it from a different perspective.

When the biblical authors speak of their experience, they do not put forward arguments concerning the processes of knowing, of learning or of judgment. It is more a question of language than anything else: burnt lips, a book which is eaten, I do not know how to speak. Inspired activity in the Bible is not presented as *charisma* of judgment but of language. We do not proclaim the 'Idea of God' but rather the 'Word of God', because, first and foremost, Scripture transmits the divine word, the communicative will of God to human beings. For humans, the genuine normal instrument of intercommunication is language, and God accepts it. If we say that the Bible is the inspired word, we affirm that it belongs in the realm of language; the biblical authors carry out a task with the tool of language. Just like any other writers, they have to elaborate a human experience in order to make it communicable. The writers carry out an activity; in the Greek tradition, this activity is *poiesis* (action) and the result is the *poiema* (act, work).

Poets are people of words who pour vital experiences into oral or written language. Their task is to transform human experience into a literary system of words. For Christians, who consider the Bible to be the Word of God, the Spirit of God intervenes when the sacred author gives the form of words to the experience that he wishes to make communicable.

Summary. The treatise of hermeneutics has a relationship of correlativity with that of biblical inspiration. Inspiration may be understood from the point of view of intellectual judgment. This brings as possible consequences the obsessive preoccupation with biblical inerrancy, fundamentalism, the ahistoricity of the text and indifference towards literary forms. Practical judgment was added to intellectual theoretical judgment. I prefer to approach the theme of inspiration from the perspective of language; the Spirit inspires authors when the latter give the form of words to the vital experience they want to communicate.

3. *Language and Inspiration*

Language is the great medium of interpersonal communication. Within this communicative relationship lies the *charisma* of inspiration, which is a *charisma* of language.

We have to conceive all the processes that give rise to language[1] as taking place under the action of the Spirit. The *charisma* resides mainly in the mission of the sacred authors to transform human experience into words, to present as written language the history of the people, their personal experiences, the significance of history, the works of salvation, and that people's reply to God. Inspiration is a *charisma* of language, and language is forged in this phase, oral or written. Before this activity, words do not exist—there is no Word of God. If the Bible is the Word of God, it is because the Spirit has directed the process.

Inspiration is a *charisma* of the Spirit which moves the human author in the process of transforming human experience into words, in such a way that the result is the work of language of the writer or author and is consecrated as the Word of God.

The definition and description offered by Monsignor Neóphytos Edelby at the Second Vatican Council fit perfectly here. He makes explicit a modern presentation of inspiration in the name of Eastern tradition:

> We would like to propose the testimony of the Eastern Churches... Our Orthodox brothers will recognise our purest common faith in this testimony.
>
> *First principle:* The mission of the Holy Spirit cannot be separated from the Word made man.
>
> *Second principle:* The Writings are a liturgical and prophetic reality... In them the Eastern Churches see *the consecration of the history of salvation under the species of human words,* inseparable from the eucharistic consecration, which sums up all the history in the body of Christ.
>
> *Third principle:* Tradition is the epiclesis of the history of salvation, the theophany of the Holy Spirit, without which the history is incomprehensible and the Scripture is empty words.

---

1 . Cf. L. Alonso Schökel, *The Inspired Word* (New York: Herder & Herder, 1965), pp. 209-13.

That is to say, the history of salvation is consecrated in the form of words, and I may communicate—enter in communion—with it just as I commune with Christ in the consecrated bread and wine. Just as the Word was made man by the shadow of the Spirit on Mary (Lk. 1.35), confirming the epithet 'holy', so the fact is expressed in words under the Spirit, and is sacred.

The ardent consecration of the lips of Isaiah, the placing of words in the mouth of Jeremiah, the written scroll eaten and assimilated by Ezekiel, the uncontrollable fire in the bones of Jeremiah, the hand that holds, the wind that snatches away—all are images of the action of the Spirit directed to the production of the word.

This does not mean that an inert reality is produced, for the book as such is no more than the mechanical and conventional notation of the word. It is a written record which conserves the word in a stable and transmissible way. This is not to deny that the activity of writing may influence the composition and expression. The words must sound again, become words again, once again be consecrated by the action of the Spirit, once again present the events in the history of salvation as revelation.

The Church invokes the Spirit to return over the bread, over the written words, eternally repeating the consecration, renewing the revelation of the acts, thus leading the Church to the plenitude of truth. The Spirit responds to this invocation or epiclesis of the Church and gradually gives it increasing spiritual knowledge of the Scripture.

In order to read a text, the ideal is to be able to share the same spirit in which it is produced. But those who do not share this situation also have access to the message registered in the text because many ways of reading a literary work exist. For the Christian, the Bible is the Word of God. We have seen the believers' vision of Scripture and the necessity to participate in the same Spirit with which it was written in order to penetrate deeply its reality as the divine-human word. However, for an unbeliever, the reality of the Bible is offered as universal literature, making different types of reading possible: lay, ethical, literary, and others. The Bible stands open for everyone who approaches it.

Chapter 3

FROM AUTHOR-HERMENEUTICS TO TEXT-HERMENEUTICS

If we wanted to characterize the ultimate hermeneutical turn in a schematically incisive manner, we would use a simple opposition: author-hermeneutics versus text-hermeneutics.

A distinction as simple as this may be used as a primary guideline. The conciliar constitution *Dei Verbum* expressed the hermeneutical principle of the *intentio auctoris* as the point of departure for critical biblical exegesis, although it leaves a door conspicuously open to 'what God meant with his words' (*DV* 12). Going through the open door, we venture along a road that leads on, and very soon we arrive at another station: 'what the text means'. The text-hermeneutics I am going to put forward does not attempt to oust the authors, but to integrate them with other factors active in the interpretative act. As we shall see, it is not correct to understand text-hermeneutics as an exact substitute for author-hermeneutics, where the primacy of the text would replace that of the author. Author, text, and others, are joint factors in an ample universe: they are correlative elements involved in a single whole, where other decisive factors coexist in literary interpretation.

1. *Author-Hermeneutics*

When we come face to face with a text, what do we want to understand and explain? The author's experience? The text as the author's objectivation? My existence at a critical juncture? This is a problem that seriously divides the opinions of the exegetes. Schleiermacher insists on the author, so much so that he goes as far as saying that, in order to understand a text, we must enter the author's mind, and identify ourselves with them, Dilthey talks of attaining total experience (*Erlebnis*)—of repeating the global experience of the author within ourselves and entering all the author's feelings (emotional, passional, etc.); and Gunkel invites the exegete, the interpreter, actually to enter the mind of the author.

a. *The Intention of the Author*
From this point of view, the sense of the text is defined by the intention of the author. In order to understand the text, the reader must understand what the author wants to say, because the key to interpretation is the intention of the author.

It is the reader's task to explain the sense which the author has given to the text. The sense is something wanted or intended by the author; not simply a datum of the text, nor something which is simply at the mercy of the reader-interpreter.

I admit that the author's intention should be considered as the first hermeneutical principle; but should it also be seen as the only principle? In order to understand a text, is it sufficient to understand the author's intention? Does this intention provide and delimit the totality of the meaning of the text, and does it assure my objectivity? Is it a criterion of validity and truth? The author's intention is a great principle, but is by no means the only principle.

What is the author's intention? It is important not to confound different positions on this when speaking of the author's intention. Intention is the same as purpose or the will to signify. The author's intention may be made clear with the following oppositions: '*vis verbi/voluntas significandi*', '*decir/querer decir*', 'say/mean', '*sagen/meinen*'. By means of a word, I express the concept I want to signify, and the object that is referred to by that concept. It is the *voluntas significandi* of the author.

This distinction is best illustrated in extraordinary cases. It often happens that persons talking in a foreign language of which they are not master, best appreciate the distance that exists between what they *are* saying and what they *want* to say. This occurs especially because, in the mother tongue, they know the word for the concept which they cannot manage to translate. If the native interlocutors are intelligent, they also appreciate that distance, and may even know how to get round the difficulty mentally and verbally. For example, a foreigner who needs some scissors asks for them in a shop in Italy and says he wants to buy a *forchetta* (a fork; he has made a mistake, he means *forbici*) there is a difference between what he says and what he means. Or think of the tourist in Spain who, on suffering some minor embarrassment, says 'Estoy embarazada', thinking they are saying 'I'm embarrassed',

but actually saying 'I'm pregnant'. It even happens that we express ourselves badly when talking to people who share the same language, so
that, in a conversation, the perplexed interlocutor asks us courteously:
'Do you mean that...?' or corrects us: 'I suppose you really mean...';
or formulates expressions such as 'I don't know if I've understood
properly', or 'what I mean is...'

A word may have a broad signifying capacity: it is what the Romans
used to call the *vis verbi* (not the *force*, but rather the *meaning* of the
word that I may find in a dictionary). Of all the various meanings of
a word, I choose one because I want to express something concrete,
which is the *voluntas significandi*.

The concept is expressed in the word, but the same word may respond to various concepts. For example, 'root' may refer to different
concepts. It does not mean the same for a dentist as for a mathemati-
cian, or for a philosopher or an agriculturist. 'Bank' conjures up different concepts in an economist, a gardener, and so on.

b. *Semantic Intention*

By intention I mean the scholastic *intentio*, the *tendere in*, the mental
movement towards, the act by which the human intellect tends towards,
directs itself to an object.

When people have an object in front of them, they perform a perception. That perception of the object is transformed into a concept which
is expressed in words. The concept is a reality that comes from the intellectual act of 'directing itself toward' something (*tendit in*): the mind
'tends towards' an object and the concept thus comes into being. We
can see it in a diagram:

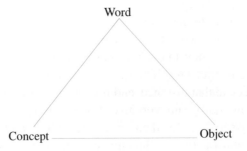

The word expresses the concept which the perception of the object
provokes in me. That conceptual expression, that signifying of a concept

by a word is an intellectual act that proceeds from the 'directing myself toward'. Thus the word refers to the object via the concept.

I may use the same word for ten concepts, but I mean only one of them. The author, who *tendit in*, is the one who decides this particular meaning. The critical work in a text is that of recovering the meaning the author wants from among several possibilities. In a similar way, a concept may be expressed with different words.

All we have said up to now as regards words may also be applied to sentences. The same expression may be made affirmative, interrogative, ironical, etc. Let us take the case of Mt. 6.22-23 where the author uses the expressions *opthalmós ponerós* and *opthalmós haplous*. Some authors translate the former as 'sick eye'. But we must consider that *ponerós* indicates an ethical dimension, so it cannot be 'sick eye'. From here we are being shown that 'eye' is being construed along different lines, that the intention of the author must be sought, and that the author has placed this expression in an antithesis that must be grasped globally. Let us come to the second formulation. *Haplous* means 'simple', both in the physical and moral sense, but here we must incline ourselves to the moral aspect since the word forms part of the antithesis. It means 'generous eye', which, in the biblical sense, leads us to 'simple heart'. But there is more, because the author is Semitic; we have to go to Hebrew in order to find a more precise meaning, because, in this case, the author's intention is conditioned by the Hebrew language. Referring to eye, *ra'a* means 'miserly' and *tob* means generous, because, for a Semite, the eye, apart from being the seat of the visual sense, is the seat of estimative valuation. So the author has used a play on words and an idiomatic expression.

By intention, in *ordinary* language, we understand what is meant (*voluntas significandi*), not what the words in themselves say. In legal and judicial language, we, or rather, judges and lawmakers, understand what was meant by those who promulgated a certain law, the *voluntas legislatorum*. The *vis verbi* is distinguished from the *voluntas legislatoris*; since a law is an act of will defined for the common good, in many cases the letter of the law is surpassed by appealing to the will of the legislator. By intention in *rhetorical* language (every form of literary language), we understand the move, seen or surmised, from what the author says to what the author means, through stylistic devices. In rhetorical language, literary tropes and figures must be taken into account.

c. *The Intention of the Author: A Critical Hermeneutical Principle*

Going into author-hermeneutics involves discussing other qualities of philosophical positivistic inspiration, namely the ideals of objectivity and precision. In author-hermeneutics, it is understood that the author consciously objectifies their thoughts—what they mean—in a given text: it is the sense of that text. This objectified meaning thus remains immutable and totally fixed; after a time the reader will look for this objectivation. The meaning of the text is there, complete, concluded, perfect; the reader's task is to reach it. The interpreter aims to establish the meaning of the text before him with complete objectivity and precision, reducing it to the author's intention. The text is thus the immediate object of study, and the meaning of the text is the goal of interpretation. The author is not an object, but the author's thoughts have been objectified in the text and are thus perfectly recoverable.

This ideal of objectivity is a beautiful thing, but it lays a trap, because it is based on a radical distinction between subject and object (reader–text), without taking into consideration the fact that in understanding, the subject is involved (otherwise would not be the subject). Objectivity is opposed to subjectivity and places all the reader's subjectivity in parentheses. Thus, in the intellect the reader must control all prejudice; in volition and emotion, all partiality, and in imagination, all anticipation. These three elements (prejudice, partiality and anticipation) must be abolished, because the reader must attain pure objectivity. With a discipline of constant renunciation and vigilance, the interpreter will treat the object of study objectively, namely the meaning of the text as intended by the author.

This principle of objectivity is to be qualified by the scientific ideal of precision. Precision is opposed to vagueness and approximation. In order to achieve this ideal, the interpreter, or rather, the philologist, elaborates methods of analysis which he treats as precision instruments. Philology is designed to be a precision instrument; not only does it want to define what the author meant, but also to do so with precision. However, what if the author did not set out to write with precision? This ideal of precision is appropriate for author-hermeneutics because it claims that meaning is in the text. So, as philology is the instrument we use to understand and determine exactly what the author meant, we shall not reject that instrument.

d. *Criticism of Author-Hermeneutics*

The most important thing for author-hermeneutics is to discover the intention of the author, known or anonymous, or at least his literary school or his period. This type of hermeneutics applied exclusively to literary texts brings the following conclusions:

1. *Neutrality*. By dint of avoiding prejudices, passions and fantasies, we convert a rich text into an irrelevant one. Total impartiality leads to an exegesis that is so aseptic and clinical that, in the end, it is of no consequence—it is interesting, but inconsequential.

2. *Distance*. In the biblical field, when exegesis is ended (at the level of the theological faculty), the pastor then takes the text and tries to apply it to the community, and is unsuccessful. Scholarly study is in danger of drawing away from life (catechism, predication, homily ...), and so scholarly exegesis is of no service to the community because they are two separate worlds. Following such a course in the literary field, we would be left with only the facts and information we have been able to obtain from the text, without ever fully understanding it.

3. *Minimalism and maximalism*. Let us take an example from an author, framing him in his period and his literary style: St Augustine, whose spiritual home was clearly the Bible. Faced with a text from St Augustine, I wonder: How do I know that here he is referring to a passage from the prophet Hosea? If I do not know, I am not entitled to propound such an interpretation as the meaning of the text. Following consistently this line of doubting, minimalism is reached in literary interpretation. However, if I know St Augustine, his literary style and his manner of using the Bible, how do I know that he is *not* referring to a passage from the prophet Hosea? Thus, for fear of missing something, I will expound it with reserve. This is a way to maximalism in literary interpretation.

We thus approach the matter of proof: we must succeed in ascertaining the authentic meaning of the text, and the usual question arises: 'How do you know the author meant that?', to which one may counter: 'And how do you know he did not mean it?' It is prejudicial and taking a predetermined option to choose the first question and ignore the second. If I ask both questions, I may then look for more information to help me; such as the author's habits or the type of text. For example, in John's Gospel (a book fond of symbols and subtle delicate allusions), I may presume with great probability that the author meant the symbol, because this is John's style. I may also suppose it is so because of the genre. Other examples could be Ruben Darío, influenced by the French symbolists, or Quevedo influenced by Seneca. If we do not ask the second question we may miss a great deal of meaning.

If the meaning is adequately defined by the author (in order to define the text I must know the author's intention, and we have to prove his intention in each case), we must unfortunately be satisfied with very little. Perhaps the author had one aspect in mind but I cannot responsibly affirm it: what I can say with certainty is very little and limited. The result is a minimalism of contents. Let us take the case of the date of a text or an author. We set the probable date in the fifth century BCE; from there we go on to say that the date could be in the second half of the fifth century BCE but less probably; and finally, as improbable but possible, we set it in the last decade of the fifth century BCE. This is the golden rule: greater precision means less probability.

Paradoxically, while being constantly bound to minimalism and being governed by its rules, we still have the immense area of conjecture and insufficiently founded hypothesis. The following principle rules: the number of hypotheses is inversely proportional to the number of known data; the fewer facts we know, the greater number of hypotheses are possible.

Summary. According to author-hermeneutics, the meaning of a text is adequately defined by the author's intention; the interpreter should strive to an ideal of objectivity and precision. This type of hermeneutics runs the risk of falling into neutrality, distance and minimalism of content and maximalism of conjectures. The author's intention is not the only and exclusive hermeneutical principle.

2. Limits of Author-Hermeneutics

In author-hermeneutics, we are listening to the ideals of the natural sciences—objectivity and precision—which grant the knowledge and command of natural forces and processes. I do not declare the theory of author-hermeneutics to be false, only limited, since it is based on limiting presuppositions.

a. The Author
According to this theory, the meaning of the text flows through the conscious and intentional act of the intellect: 'I mean this and nothing

else'. Whatever does not pass through the reflective conscience of the author is not the meaning of the text.

But this cannot be affirmed from the historic reality of how one reads, of how books are transmitted in the millennial tradition of humanity. The text is full of meaning that comes from desire, from fantasy, from the author's subconscious, and which is indeed part of the meaning of the text, but which does not pass through the reflective activity of the author's intellect. The author's psychology is far more complex than that of a scheme of intention in meaning.

In an author, can we say that conscious intention is everything? Does it explain everything? What about fantasy, intuition, emotivity, desire? It is fictitious to reduce the author to the mechanism of intention; it is inventing what does not exist. Modern psychology compels us to a more complex vision of the literary creator, of the author.

We have a nice example in the great vision of Ezek. 37.1-14: the vision of the dry bones. Ezekiel is a prophet and a priest, and a man full of hope, preoccupied with the repatriation of his people; for him it is vital to return to the homeland and recover the land. He composes the vision of the dry bones. What does Ezekiel mean with this most beautiful poem? He tells us immediately afterwards. We then realize that Ezekiel has grasped only a small part of the sense of his symbol. Its significant richness surpasses him, because Ezekiel has a historical and a cultural constraint that has not allowed Ezekiel the exegete to comprehend Ezekiel the poet. He has not understood his own text because he is limited by a historical and cultural setting determined by two factors: repatriation and disbelief in the resurrection of the dead. Ezekiel has prophetically created a magnificent symbol whose meaning lies beyond him when he tries to explain it. The historical–cultural filter has prevented him from going further in the comprehension of his own work. If we remove the historical–cultural filter, we know and believe that the resurrection is a fact in Christ. Ezekiel has created a symbol of new life.

In this poem, desire has slipped through an underground channel, stealthily bypassing the conscious will of the author. The deep-rooted human desire for life, the desire to believe that not everything is to end here, has become word in Ezekiel's poem. Ezekiel the critic has not understood Ezekiel the poet. He did not comprehend the reach of his symbol because he did not get to its roots, but he gave it a poetic form and left it to his successors: it is his imperishable merit.

In the name of objectivity we may say that author-hermeneutics is not objective. It does not respond. It does not work. It is based on an *a priori* which goes against the experience of what a literary author is.

b. *The Work/Text*
If we take the reality of the literary work as such, we observe that it is a system of significant forms and relationships. A sonnet is not 14 propositions placed one after another, but rather a unity. And it is a significant unity that is not purely formal. Each phrase significantly influences the totality and vice versa.

Relationships not planned by the author come into being in the act of writing or developing a work. New relationships are brought to light by a situation or a character. This is even more so if we think about what in the work is symbolic or could be symbolic—symbolic in such a way that the author may not have understood all its potentiality.

The work goes beyond the author. From the point of view of the work, author-hermeneutics is insufficient. The work will not remain enclosed in a historical moment; the work goes further than the author. It may even be converted into a 'symbol of'. Cervantes did not realize that his character Don Quixote is a symbol of a human type and contains the complete process of how to be one type of man, simply because Cervantes was immersed in a definite cultural milieu. We have another example in Franz Kafka with his *Metamorphosis*. Did he get to understand all the force of his symbol of the man oppressed by a culture in which he is reduced to an insect, as well as the force of the crude realism with which he himself expressed it?

c. *The Reader/Listener*
If we take the part of the reader, the ideal of objectivity is a sophism, because, where there is a subject, there is subjectivity.

It is impossible to observe without being part of the process. It is useless to say that it is seen without somebody looking. It is impossible to look from 'nowhere', because, in order to be able to see, an angle of vision is necessary. Objectivity rejects that angle, which would be the same as placing oneself 'nowhere' and looking from there. I do not mean that objectivity is not possible, but that it comes in degrees, and that pure objectivity does not exist. It is always related to the subjectivity of the person who perceives, receives and grasps the surrounding reality.

In order to contemplate a painting, I must place myself in some position or other with a certain angle. There are pictures that have to be seen from below or from one side: in others I may choose my viewpoint. But on getting myself into position, I am getting the painting into position. Insofar as the painting is a manifestation, its appreciation is affected by the position and posture of the contemplator. The stained-glass windows of a Gothic cathedral may be seen well only from the interior of the building. The same thing happens when the reader comes face to face with a text. Therefore we also see how, from the perspective of the reader, author-hermeneutics is insufficient.

3. *Teaching of the Church*

A specific case of what we have said up to now could be the believer's explanation of the Bible. In the latest version of ecclesiastical teachings, what is the hermeneutical principle applied to Holy Scripture by the Second Vatican Council?

At the time when the Council's text was discussed, author-hermeneutics predominated almost exclusively among Catholics, so that it was to be expected that this form of critical reading of the Bible would be canonized in the *Dei Verbum* constitution. The original text said: *Cum autem Deus in Sacra Scriptura per homines more hominum locutus sit* (*DV* 12). 'God having spoken in Holy Scripture through humanity and in the human way.' It is a fact of human language. It is human beings who speak (*langue*) and they do so in the way of humans (*parole*). This is the first theological principle: to take the incarnation of God and God's Word seriously. Let us see where the hermeneutical principle comes in:

> Interpretation of Holy Scripture: *Interpretes Sacrae Scripturae, ut perspiciat, quid Ipse nobiscum communicare voluerit, attente investigare debet quid hagiographi reapse significare intenderint et eorum verbis manifestare Deo placuerit* (*Dei Verbum* 12). So that the interpreter of Holy Scripture may understand what God wanted to communicate to us, he must conscientiously investigate what the hagiographers really wanted to express.

In order to understand the revealed meaning, it is necessary to pass through what the sacred writer means. Up to there, author-hermeneutics seems to be established.

But further on, *et eorum verbis manifestare Deo placuerit* is added: in order to know what God wanted to communicate, it is necessary to know not only what the author meant but also what God wanted to say with the words of the author (*eorum verbis*), that is, the text.

The Council opens a door of interpretation. It has not closed hermeneutics in with the author's intention, because, having arrived at this point, the conciliar fathers have realized that, with the actual words, God eventually wanted to say things of which the author was not conscious.

Summary. Author-hermeneutics is limited. In the author, fantasy, intuition, emotivity and so on, must be reckoned with. The literary work is a system of significant relationships that go beyond its author. In the reader, objectivity is possible to a degree, but where there is a subject there is subjectivity. A particular case of the explication of hermeneutical principles is to be found in the Second Vatican Council regarding the interpretation of Holy Scripture: it asserts the importance of the author's intention, and also of the text as a relatively autonomous significant reality.

I began this theme affirming that the latest hermeneutical trend is marked by the hermeneutical opposition of author-hermeneutics to a text-hermeneutics. I have expounded the limits of author-hermeneutics and of the exclusivity of the author's intention in literary interpretation. Text-hermeneutics, which is the hermeneutics I propose, includes the theme of the author's intention, while emphasizing the fact that this alone is insufficient.

Understanding by 'intention' the conscious act by which the mind turns towards its object (*mens tendit in*), in the reading of the literary work we find a convergence of two subjects that are mentally conscious of the same objects. The readers escape from the empirical world and become the subjects of another world of objects. The readers are surprised to find themselves full of thoughts, images and feelings that they constitute as objects, and which in turn belong to another: 'When my person is strangely invaded by the thoughts of another, I am that I who is allowed to think the thoughts of others'.[1]

---

1.   George Poulet, quoted in W. Ray, *Literary Meaning: From Phenomenology to Deconstruction* (Oxford: Basil Blackwell, 1985), p. 10.

The literary work appears to us as a complex of relationships in which diverse factors exist related to each other. It is necessary to bear in mind all these factors which are included in the literary work and which we are now going to study in detail. The literary work is communication. On the one hand, we have someone who transmits a message that is received by another subject. It is an interesting threesome: (1) an author who says (2) something to (3) a reader. This communicative activity is developed on very specific bases—the author elaborates the work on a concrete subject matter, that is to say, develops a theme. And, on the other hand, there is one more factor to analyse in the literary complex, for the author elaborates the text using an indispensable instrument for that activity: language.

Chapter 4

THE HISTORICAL-CRITICAL METHOD

1. *Introduction*

As we pass from author-hermeneutics to text-hermeneutics (in the sense explained above) it seems useful to reflect on the historical-critical method as it is practised today, because it is the chief representative of author-hermeneutics. This fact alone does not lead me to reject this method which has so many merits, but simply to direct a few criticisms against it.

This method aims at understanding texts in their coordinates of space and time, of which culture is a principal factor. This method is not used specifically because texts deal with historical facts—since the method is also applied to lyric or dramatic texts—but because it considers that the meaning of the text was conditioned by the specific historical setting in which it appeared. However, conditioned is not the same as determined—texts are not the necessary products of physical causes. However, authors do not operate in a total vacuum, free from all conscious or unconscious influence. Identical circumstances can produce both a response and its opposite, one positive and one negative. For example, in a circumstance in which a decision is being made (2 Sam. 17.1-16), one counsellor (Achitophel) suggests a lightning action against David while the other (Husay) advises that they prepare the battle slowly and on a large scale, but both are conditioned by the same problem, even though they have opposing loyalties. And again, in Micah 4–5 we listen to different and even opposing concepts, but both are conditioned by the idea of a restoration under the sign of David.

Among the conditioning factors, the one which bears the most weight seems to be culture (understood in a generous sense). When conditions change in time, space and culture, there consequently develops a distance between reader and text. The historical-critical method tries to bridge this distance by travelling to the past (and not bringing the text to the present).

Applying this to the Bible, we affirm that the texts are old: The Old Testament with respect to the New Testament and the New Testament with respect to us. Biblical texts are not ahistorical entities, inhabitants of a rarefied atmosphere, floating without ballast in a limbo that is always accessible. The historical-critical method makes an effort to recover or reconstruct the specific historical conditions under which the texts appeared, with the purpose of understanding and explaining them. It set out to do this in a systematically controllable way, in other words, scientifically.

The historical-critical method is fully justified and has produced excellent results in its entirety. It responds to the historical condition of the texts. It has accumulated and put at our disposal an incalculable and growing knowledge of past cultures, and educated us to comprehend texts in their historical context. It supplies us with a complete set of valuable instruments. It would be an enormous loss not to use the historical-critical method. But it and its supporters are also conditioned. It would be a major inconsistency to consider this method as an absolute and thus to exempt it from the need for self-criticism. By pointing out some of its limitations and uncovering some of its presuppositions, the historical-critical method can continually be refined and enriched.

2. *Limits of the Historical-Critical Method*

In the first place, we must consider that the force of conditions is different according to the type of text.

1. First and foremost comes the world of *everyday life*: elements such as family, the human life cycle, work in the fields, and so on. Psalm 136 is exemplary: it devotes four participles to the cosmic action of God, another four to his historical action in the liberation of the people, gathers a series of incidents in a brief formula, and concludes, affirming that 'he gives bread to all living beings'. In other words, it leaps from history to everyday life, alongside which history slides at a tangent.

The world of proverbs enters fully at this point. For example: the door turns on its hinges, the lazy one in his bed (Prov. 25.14). Does this have a date? The fact that that lazy one does not have a spring mattress does not impede comprehension of this proverb. Sayings travel through space, time and culture but are impeded by them. The more academic ones may show signs of a cultured elaboration, but this does not affect the substance. The best ones remain fresh throughout time and history.

Something similar may be said about *elemental sentiments*: fear, joy, satisfaction, desire. It is only individual aberration on the part of one supporter or other of the historical-critical method to say that we cannot understand the anguish of a mother in the difficult moment of giving birth, without bearing in mind the historical conditions. *Nequid nimis!* Don't go too far!

2. There is also *the typical* as opposed to what is individual. By definition, the historical fact is unique—it happens only once. Many human actions are typical, that is, reducible to a type that is little affected by historical events. The wedding of a king, any king, is typical, conditioned perhaps by belonging to the Davidian dynasty, but not individually because of being King N. In the explanation of the psalms there are often two opposed schools: those that seek the individual unique situation, and those that look for a typical situation. Some psalms offer data that refer to an individual historical moment; the majority, however, are valid for a typical situation (e.g. a sick person, a fugitive). Gunkel successfully defended the typical situation of the majority of the Psalms, as opposed to old historifying titles or equivalent modern attempts. Normally, what is typical is also a historical category, for example, the cult of Israel. But history affects it only at a certain distance.

3. A variant of the two preceding aspects comes under the heading of *cyclic*, subtracted in great measure from the linearity inherent in all that is historical. Ecclesiastes meditates on the cyclical character of natural phenomena and, in their likeness, of human events:

> The sun rises, the sun sets, it gasps for breath as it struggles to reach its place and then leaves it once more... One generation goes, another generation comes, while the earth remains quiet (1.5.4)

The anonymous author is conditioned by the time (doubtful), by a school, to look critically with certain scepticism at the changes in history: 'What has happened will happen; what occurred will occur: there is nothing new under the sun' (1.9) (and this author was very new to biblical culture and literature).

4. Finally, a patently historical *individual factor*. There are parts of the human spirit that overcome the conditions of history to the point of shaping them; that soar to a greater height from which they can then contemplate history. There are those brilliant characters that condition

history rather than allowing it to condition them. Such geniuses are certainly historical characters, but when the historical-critical method comes across them, it should not ignore their geniality or reduce them to the influences and conditions under which they existed.

Another aspect, bound to what goes before, is that the historical process is not strictly linear like a chain of causes and effects. If, when looking from a certain distance or from a good height, we may distinguish phases and perhaps an evolutionary design, on approaching more closely we discover examples of anticipation, delay, temporary coexistence of disparate positions, and so on. A far-seeing mind that anticipates the future is acting in the same year as another lazy mind that drags the past along. The historical-critical method must beware of falling into the temptation of dividing texts into bands of perfectly homogenous thought.

If we now pay attention to the practice of comprehension and explanation, we observe that the first thing is, frequently, to comprehend the sense of a text, and the second, to seek a historical situation in which it fits. Comprehension goes before; the historical explanation of the coordinates in which it may have appeared is added to it. This proves that some comprehension of the text exists before its historical genesis is known. If we know beforehand the circumstances in which it came into being, so much the better; but this should not be exaggerated, as if historical-critical comprehension were the only way to comprehend, or the only scientific way.

The better practioners of this method keep in mind these limits of their cognitive instrument. These who are only average need to have these limits pointed out to them, as they are not apparently obvious to them. It is the task of hermeneutics to bring the presuppositions of the interpretative practice to the surface.

In the collections of prophetic oracles, especially in the book of Jeremiah, we observe that some oracles are presented or set in the framework of their historical circumstances. Others are collected with absolutely no historical reference. This tells us that the collectors attribute unequal value to the historical conditions of each oracle, and that difference in attitude is also a historical fact.

Summary. The historical-critical method exerts itself to recover or reconstruct the specific historical conditions under which texts were produced, with the aim of understanding and explaining their meaning. It wishes to do so in a controllable, systematic and, thus, scientific way. However, it has some limits: the power of conditions is diverse according to the type of text; the historical process is not strictly linear; very often, the first thing is to comprehend the sense of a text, and the second is to seek a setting in which to fit it.

3. *The Historical-Critical Method and its Explanation by Causes*

In the world of nature, where determinism prevails (albeit as a statistical generality), phenomena are explained by their causes; causes inherent in the partial or total system (without having recourse to metaphysical causes, which act at another level). In the cultural world, where human imagination and freedom are active, explanation of phenomena by causes has a limited scope. Explanation is not simply defining the phenomenon in question as the effect of causes, but rather grasping and explaining the meaning of human acts or texts.

In spite of everything, the causal factor does indeed have an important role to play in a complex organism. The causal factor of the texts may be condensed into two elements: the author and the author's influences. It is useful to give proper value to the causal factor, but also to be aware of its limits.

a. *The Author.*

Is it necessary (or even important) to know the author in order to comprehend a text? It depends—there is no universal answer. Is Paul the author of the letter to the Hebrews? No critical exegete defends this today. Is the author of the Apocalypse the same as that of John's Gospel? The majority deny it. Today no one defends the idea that the author of Isaiah 40–55 is the Isaiah of the eighth century, that Moses wrote the Pentateuch, that David was the author of many psalms, that Solomon wrote the Greek book of Wisdom.

It is undoubtedly easier to understand, and far better to explain the complex Isaiah 40–55 if we assume it to be the work of a prophet during the Babylonian exile. It would not be out of place to remember controversies and prohibitions at the end of the nineteenth century and the beginning of the twentieth.

Knowing the author does not necessarily mean knowing the author's name. It is more important to know their historical and cultural milieux; we may replace the name by a symbol. Deutero-Isaiah or Second Isaiah is called the Prophet of Exile; the difficult name of 'the Deuteronomist' has been coined; for some decades we had a 'Yahwhist' (who is today leading a precariously threatened existence in scholarship).

Let us take the case of Jesus Ben Sira. Knowing his name and surname does not help us much to comprehend his book: but it is interesting to place it (according the Greek prologue) in the peaceful period between the tolerance edict of Antioch III (200 BCE) and the persecution of Antioch IV Epiphanes (175–163 BCE). It is also interesting to incorporate it into sapiential circles (*hakamim*) devoted to studying the law and Scripture, which had already been constituted at the time; but we are only able to obtain these data from his book once the book is understood.

We thus arrive at the first limitation. Frequently, and nearly always in dealing with ancient texts, we do not understand the text starting from the author (the effect from the cause), but we deduce or guess at the author's profile from the book which is now understood. We also have the legitimate circular (or spiral) process: from the book which is partly understood, we gather a partial image of the author. This allows us to understand the text more exactly, which allows us to better profile the author, and so on.

The importance of knowing the author in order to comprehend the text must not be exaggerated. Let us remember the lively discussions over whether the author of *Macbeth* and *Hamlet* was really Shakespeare or Marlowe or an anonymous genius of the same period. We have been spared discussions regarding Cervantes; but there are plenty with respect to Fernando de Rojas and La Celestina (The Madam), not to mention the author of *Viaje a Turquía* ('Journey to Turkey'). In biblical scholarship, disproportionate efforts are devoted to guessing at the authors of works or parts of them.

Ancient authors had a different mentality from ours: they neither reserved copyright nor were they paid royalties, they copied and adapted unscrupulously, they did not disdain the fictive author nor pseudonymity. It could be more desirable to have resort to an illustrious name than to immortalize one's own. How many modern authors would feel proud to sign some of the psalms or the so-called book of Ecclesiastes?

Among the ancients, says Gunkel,[1] tradition and convention had more weight; but he does not deny the existence of brilliant creative authors. There are many brilliant pages in prophetic literature.

1. H. Gunkel, *Reden und Aufsätze* (Gottingen: Vandenhoeck & Ruprecht, 1913).

b. *Influences.*

Another way of explaining a text by causes is to go back from the text itself to what influenced it, and to what factors it depended on, an operation which is both useful and limited. We probably find it easier to understand and explain St John of the Cross going up through Sebastián de Córdoba to Garcilaso; much of our fifteenth-century lyric poetry is explained in the light of Petrarch and Petrarchism. The identification of sources and influences is a common practice that has also penetrated biblical research and has given excellent results, but it must not be exaggerated.

Influences are substantially like tributaries that penetrate into the channel of the new literary work and join its current. Their relationships with the new work may be of opposing signs: they may impose their meaning on the text, or may be absorbed by the new work, with a change of meaning.

Job quotes a phrase from Psalm 8: 'What is man that you make much of him and turn your thoughts toward him?' (7.17), altering its meaning; doing the same by making morning into a time of grace. It is essential to recognize the reference in order to appreciate the author's violent operation: 'it is in this way that Job, and the poet, uses traditional venerable texts, to draw a new meaning from them'.[2]

The New Testament freely uses the Old Testament in the form of adapted or commented quotations, or taken as a nucleus to be freely developed, as a quarry or mine of symbols, as a mint for the coining of formulas. The exegetes of the New Testament know this very well. In general, the quotations have been well studied, but there remains much to be done in terms of references to symbols, formulas and models.

Gospel experts have the enormous advantage of having three well-defined versions of the same events, together with related parts in the fourth Gospel. This allows them to reconstruct probable oral or written sources and to define organically what is peculiar to each Gospel.

For anyone who ventures into the Old Testament, the operation is much more difficult due to our (barely confessed) ignorance of the chronology of the texts. Starting from the Old Testament, sources and influences are sought in the surrounding literature of Egypt, Mesopotamia, Canaan, among others.

When seeking sources, it is not necessary to insist on a recognized principle that is to be consistently applied, but it is of interest to point

2.   L. Alonso Schökel and J.L. Sicre, *Job* (Madrid: Cristiandad, 1983), p. 162.

out the limits of this approach and the dangers of misuse. The main error is the hunt for instances of dependence to the point of dissolving the text back into its tributaries. We get so involved in the details that the main issue of the work is forgotten. Besides, the pursuit of sources obliges us to come to a halt somewhere or other. The biblical deluge story depends on the Akkadian Gilgamesh; no one doubts it. The Akkadian Gilgamesh depends on the Sumerian Ziusudra. What does the Sumerian text depend on? No one can affirm that it is the absolute beginning.

After all the influences have been identified, the new text still has to be explained. With slight changes in a love poem, St John of the Cross writes his religious poem 'El Pastorcico' ('The Little Shepherd Boy'); and the same thing happens with a great deal of poetry which is *a lo divino*. The task is to understand and explain the sense of the text, not to be content with identifying its causes, author or influences.

Summary. The causal factor of texts can be condensed into two elements: the authors and their influences. It is useful to give proper value to the causal factor, but also to be aware of its limits. We cannot be content simply with the identification of the causes, author and influences of a text.

Part II

TEXT-HERMENEUTICS

Introduction

1 CORINTHIANS 2: A HERMENEUTICAL THEORY

We have seen that author-hermeneutics shows itself to be insufficent for adequate comprehension and interpretation of the literary work. Therefore, it is preferable to venture another approach, and hence elaborate a theory that will explain and support interpretation by taking into account the diverse factors involved in it: text-hermeneutics.

Let us begin by reading a superb page from Scripture: 1 Corinthians 2. In this passage, Paul proposes wisdom (*sophia*) to a Greek audience. It is a new wisdom—God's wisdom (*sophia Theou*)—which he receives from God and which is about God. This wisdom also has a characteristic: it is hidden (*apokekrymmenen*), and is developed in a sphere of mystery (*en mysterioi*). Such wisdom that comes from and is about God is not human wisdom; neither is it metaphysical knowledge of God himself. It is about God's project, God's gift in Christ, condensed into the cross:

> We preach a crucified Messiah, a stumbling block for the Jews, foolishness for the gentiles; but for them that are called, both Jews and Greeks, a Messiah who is the power of God and the wisdom of God; for the foolishness of God is wiser than men, and the weakness of God is stronger than men (1 Cor. 1.23-25).

This is the theme, the nucleus of that wisdom. Paul refers to it in search of unity, for the Corinthians were divided, erroneously placing their faith in the evangelists from whom they had received the gospel. That is why he argues:

> My message and my preaching did not lie in wise and persuasive words, but in the demostration of the power of the Spirit, so that your faith might not stand on the wisdom of men [*in sophia anthropon*], but on the power of God [*en dynamei Theou*] (1 Cor. 2.4-5).

What is the problem Paul confronts? He must propose a transcendent wisdom to a human community of believers and non-believers, whose cosmopolitan nature harbours the class divisions of the Hellenistic–Roman period. Paul is thus mediator and interpreter for the Corinthians.

However, Paul did not attain that knowledge that he is proposing to the Corinthians through the wisdom of the world (*sophia kosmou*), for this wisdom does not reach the knowledge of God's plan. The evidence is obvious: 'if they had known it, they would not have crucified the Lord of glory' (1 Cor. 2.8).

How is this knowledge reached? By means of the Spirit (*dia tou pneumatos*) (1 Cor. 2.9). The Spirit is the mediator, the interpreter of God,

> For the Spirit explores everything even the depths of God's own nature. Who knows what a human being is but the human spirit within him? In the same way, only the Spirit of God knows what God is (1 Cor. 2.10-11).

This knowledge has come to Paul by means of the Spirit, and to the Corinthians by way of Paul. There is thus a double mediation: the mediation of the Spirit between God and Paul, and the mediation of Paul between the Spirit and the Corinthians.

Once it is made clear what the wisdom of the Christian kerygma consists of, where it comes from and through whom it reaches the faithful, Paul concerns himself with language as the *medium* by which it is transmitted:

> We speak of these gifts of God in words taught us not by our human wisdom but by the Spirit, explaining spiritual things in spiritual terms (1 Cor. 2.13).

The appropriate language is pneumatic; a pneumatic message requires a pneumatic language. Furthermore, the listener must have the pneumatical capacity to listen, over and above the *psychic* or *sarkic* capacity. The 'rational' ear will not comprehend the discourse because the discourse and the medium itself are pneumatic.

Regarding Paul's value judgment that 'The crucified one is the Messiah', if the listeners are not 'on the same wavelength', tuned in to the *Pneuma*, they will reject it as madness (*moria*, 1 Cor. 2.14). The value of the sentence should be verified by a pneumatic, not psychic, judgment:

> A simple man does not accept what proceeds from the Spirit of God for it seems madness to him; and he cannot understand it because it is perceived only spiritually (1 Cor. 2.14).

> However, we possess the mind of the Messiah (1 Cor. 2.16).

Now let us reread the text of 1 Corinthians 2, making out a hermeneutic chart:

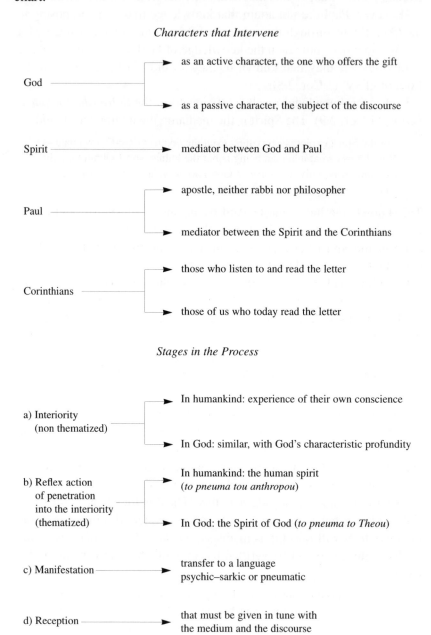

Characters that Intervene

God
- as an active character, the one who offers the gift
- as a passive character, the subject of the discourse

Spirit → mediator between God and Paul

Paul
- apostle, neither rabbi nor philosopher
- mediator between the Spirit and the Corinthians

Corinthians
- those who listen to and read the letter
- those of us who today read the letter

Stages in the Process

a) Interiority (non thematized)
- In humankind: experience of their own conscience
- In God: similar, with God's characteristic profundity

b) Reflex action of penetration into the interiority (thematized)
- In humankind: the human spirit (*to pneuma tou anthropou*)
- In God: the Spirit of God (*to pneuma to Theou*)

c) Manifestation → transfer to a language psychic–sarkic or pneumatic

d) Reception → that must be given in tune with the medium and the discourse

Paul does not adopt a hermeneutic schema 'in the human way'; he does not say: 'the Spirit has revealed to me', but rather affirms: 'the Spirit has been given to me'. Yet he does not give himself to the Corinthians, instead limiting himself to giving a message.

Here, the hermeneutic schema comes to a break in continuity, for there is no parallelism between the two mediations. Paul's way of communication with the Corinthians is not concordant with what and how he has received it. He has to make use of words that express something that was not previously pronounced.

The hermeneutic schema discovered in 1 Corinthians 2 introduces us to the exposition of my hermeneutic approach. It is fundamental to comprehend the literary work in order to interpret it. Diverse elements are coupled in the act of comprehension, and may be dealt with in many ways. The literary *work* is the product of an *author* directed to a *reader*. This communication is carried out on a *theme* in a specific *language*. We may see all this more clearly with the help of the following diagram which gathers the set of factors involved in the literary work:

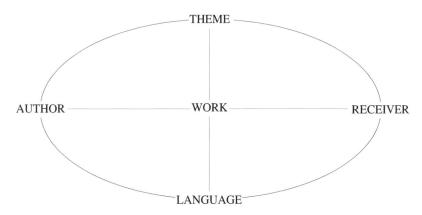

As we have opted for text-hermeneutics, the work itself occupies the centre of the diagram. The literary work is placed as the bearer of meaning between the author and the receiver (= reader). This linear relationship is mediated by the language, and proceeds concerning a theme or subject: that which is developed in the communication and evolves in a specific language.

Hermeneutics should take these factors into account in order to avoid the danger of falling into reductionist or partial interpretations. It would be a mistake to give an exclusive position to any of the elements of the diagram with detriment to the others. It is a different thing to give more importance to one factor than another, depending on the type of inter-pretative activity and the circumstances of the work (it is evident that, in a romantic poem, the author factor is more present than the others; or that, in a didactic exposition, the theme factor is very important).

What do we need to understand in order to interpret a literary work adequately? The answer is global, and so I am going to analyse it in detail making use of this schema I have proposed. First, I describe the working of the factors involved in the schema. In order to analyse the relationships of these elements I isolate them according to the follow-ing lines of relationship:

A–W–R: from the author to the receiver by way of the work
A–T–R: from the author to the receiver by way of the theme
A–L–R: language on the line from the author to the receiver
T–W–L: language on the line from the theme to the work

On each line of relationship will appear aspects that are never exclu-sive of a specific relationship (hermeneutic circle, pre-comprehension, horizon, etc.), but which, for the sake of expositional clarity, may well be included in one or other of them, normally in the one where their influence is most obvious.

Before going on to my analysis, it is advisable to remember that I am isolating factors that are not actually separated, but rather related among themselves. They are co-factors that organize a whole, and are assembled to form an organized unitary system. It is important not to lose sight of this overall perspective.

Chapter 5

THE AUTHOR–WORK–RECEIVER LINE

I begin the analysis with what seems most obvious: the line that goes from the author, through the literary work, to the receiver, and between them the literary work. The speaker sends a message to the hearer, the writer to the reader. The hearer/reader understands it or tries to understand it. Along this line, and with these three elements, some questions arise:

(1) What do I want to understand? What is the object of my interpretation? What do I need to understand in a text in order to interpret it? There are three possible answers to this question: I am interested in the author, or what I want to interpret is the text, or I may focus my interest on the readers, who understand themselves in the interpretative act.

(2) What direction does the movement take on this line? Where does its path begin and where does it go? From left to right or vice versa? Does only a unidirectional relationship exist or is the circle of relationships widened?

1. *What is the Object of Interpretation?*

a. *What Interests Me is the* Author
We want to know the author, their complexity and richness. The work simply mediates; through it we want to understand the author. The important thing is not the work but the author and the author's specific experience.

This is a type of psychologism we have already discussed. Dilthey moved on this line when he spoke of conscious human experience (*Erlebnis*). He studied the action by means of which a global fact is objectified in a literary text in the form of words. Objectified in this way, experience is transmitted to the reader, who has access to it through the text. In this way, the reader enters the psychology of the author. Comprehension, and consequently interpretation, has the author's experience as its object. In this psychologistic theory the text practically disappears; it is merely a springboard for reaching the author's experience. When the text is used, it may be forgotten.

In the biblical field we find a psychologizing version in Gunkel's project. For him the purpose of exegesis is to reach the author's unique interiority by means of the work. However, the force of literary conventions was very great in antiquity, so that the expression of the biblical author was very much bound to these conventions, which are called 'literary genres'. Faithful to his principles, Gunkel should have laid more emphasis on what is individual rather than generic, but, in practice, he became famous for and exerted influence mostly in support of his study of literary genres.

This psychologism may take us to the absolute dominion of the author's intention, in tune with a theory of inspiration which focuses on judgment. If the topic of intention and its function in speaking and writing are seen as of first importance, this may lead to a perilously narrow psychologism, where intention is declared to be the supreme and only instance of meaning.

Let us transfer this vision to biblical terms: through the text we have access to God's intention or even to God's interiority. Is this valid or admissible? We believe that, through inspiration, God is in some way author of biblical words, even if it is by means of human authors. 'May each one consider that by the tongue of prophets we listen to God who is talking to us.'[1] Through the hagiographers who composed the works, and through their constructed narrative worlds, God really speaks to us. We reach God through the work because God has become manifest in it, in a kind of incarnation. 'What is Scripture if not a letter from the omnipotent God to his creature?... Meditate diligently on the words of your Creator every day. Learn God's heart in God's words.'[2]

There is a great deal of truth in what Dilthey and Gunkel say. In a way, the author is in the work; something of the author, of the author's interior life, is communicated to us by the mediation of the text. In fact, an intersubjective encounter happens—the discovery in the text of a

1.   Chrysostom, cited in *Patrologia Graeca* 53, p. 119.
2.   Gregory the Great, cited in *Patrologia Latina* 77, p. 706.

rich personality which, in turn, enriches me. But this reality must be qualified: concrete personal experience is unique and untransferable; in the author's work, the objectivification of his experience is neither complete nor perfect. Through the work a vicarious experience arises which, in its way, repeats the author's, because experience may be passed on only analogously. This is why the most we may attain is to become enriched by a vicarious experience of the author which is transmitted by the text.[3]

b. *What Interests Me Is to Understand the* Work

That is the most objective and prevailing trend today. The literary work is born of an author, but it is an autonomous reality and is, so to speak, an adult in its own right.

The work is a precise system of orderly and significant words; it is a structure or a system of structures. As a completed structure, it is an acomplished act and at the same time a potential that demands to be realized. The work is there, available to us, inviting us to enter it and discover its multiple facets and possibilities of communication.

The work is consistent. Since it is a finished work it sustains itself, but it possesses this subsistence by its being a system of words, not precisely by its written notation. The way of recording the work is secondary. The curious and thought-provoking thing is that, to be exact, in recording the work, it is not the work that is conserved but its notation; this is why the literary work may be repeated and should be repeated, because it is a manifestation happening only when a listener or a reader creates it again. From this point of view, textual exclusivism is impossible. From what we have said, the presence of the subject who actualizes, interprets and reproduces the work is manifest: namely the reader.

c. *The Object of Interpretation Is the* Self-comprehension of the Reader

The work stimulates readers to know themselves in their authenticity or falsity. The Bible is read to understand oneself, to reform and change, to pass from falsity to existential authenticity—this is the trend represented by Bultmann, Robinson and Fuchs. Fuchs reached the point of giving the following formula: the text puts me in a situation that urges me to decide, I manifest myself in the decision, and, on manifesting myself, I understand myself. The text is but a revolving door which

3.   Cf. L. Alonso Schökel, *La palabra inspirada: La Biblia a la luz de la ciencia del lenguaje* (Madrid: Cristiandad, 3rd edn, 1986), pp. 302-305.

provokes the readers to confront themselves. The work serves to un-
mask, to find the existential truth of the readers. Since provocation is
the main issue, the text is always a happening.[4]

Bultmann presents this conception in a paradoxical way: what God
communicates cannot be objectified: the only reality is that God communicates, not what God communicates. Therefore, the Bible is not in
itself the Word of God, but it produces in me something that is the
Word of God and requires an answer. God communicates, but communicates nothing. The Bible is reactive; for Bultmann the text is an
'impact' with no concept, since its object is not to inform or say anything, but rather to provoke an answer.

It is true that, in the interpretative act, the listeners enrich and deepen
their own knowledge. It is also true that, outside oneself there exists no
neutral point where a person can meet God; only within oneself, when
one feels touched, may one find God, and the Word of God is that
touch which dispenses with the contents of a text and avoids objectivation. St John of the Cross expressed his experience of relationship with
God as 'the touch at the apex of the soul'.

The mistake here once again lies in exclusivism, in focusing everything on one's own ego. Exclusivism relegates everything else: the
Bible is not the Word of God, but rather the human reply to the Word
of God, which gives me the chance to be reached here and now by
another of God's Words, although the biblical occasion may be substituted perfectly by another text. There is thus the danger of coming to a
solipsism which shuns the community and the tradition; interpretation
becomes a self-contemplation that ignores the community and places
the individual alone before God.

'When I read a book I try to know myself.' Stated thus, this principle
sounds strange; but it holds an element of truth, especially in texts that
are very provoking. In Isa. 5.1-7 the audience listens to a vineyard
song: at a certain moment they are invited to participate, to act as a jury
in the dispute of the singer, to take sides, and not to remain impassive.
On entering this dynamic, the new reader of the poem recognizes themself as the subject and may observe their reactions, behaviour and
response to the text. The reader is manifesting herself or himself and
thus enriches self-comprehension. In the book of Deuteronomy, recourse is made to the reminiscence of the people's experience, because

---

4.   See G. Ebeling, *Word and Faith* (Philadelphia: Fortress Press, 1963).

humanity is not perfected; people must be put to the test and so people make and manifest their true self:

> Remember the way that the Lord, your God, has made you travel these forty years through the desert, to afflict you, to put you to the test and know your intentions, whether you observe his precepts (Deut. 8.2).

Summary. The literary work is the product of an author directed to a reader. This communication is carried out on a theme in a specific language. The object of the literary interpretation may be the author, the work or my self-comprehension as reader, but all three factors are actually interrelated.

2. *Direction of Movement on the Author–Work–Receiver Line*

On this line there is a movement which we immediately grasp because it is obvious to us: from the author to the work, from the work to the receiver, and from the author to the receiver. But it is not useless to analyse the direction of this movement. As we shall see, there are many important nuances in this set of related factors. The most striking is that it is difficult to define a unidirectional movement. I am trying to describe a relationship in which there is correlativity and where the elements should not be isolated, since each one spontaneously drives us to focus our attention on another of the factors. A sort of pendular dialogical movement is produced.

a. *The Movement from the Author to the Work*
The author makes a text reach the receiver. From the author to the text there is a clear relationship, a clear movement. But is there a corresponding reverse movement from the text to the author?

The literary work begins to exist first as intuition; it is a project, a very generic wish in the author's mind. Before the author's work exists, the author plans it in an ideal theoretical manner, anticipating a vision of it. This vision conditions the author; it is not yet the literary text; but something that belongs to it already exists. The work already begins to exist, and begins to act on the author in such a way that they even sometimes feel dominated by the idea. In this sense, an extreme case is that of an author who gets the idea of a group of characters with a plot, but it is not entirely to their satisfaction and they reject it; except that the idea returns time and again, until it finally imposes itself and they write it (this is the case of Pirandello's *Six Characters in Search of an*

Author, a clear example of the movement from the text towards the author). The confessions of some writers on the elaboration of a literary work are noteworthy, such as Julien Green in his memoirs or Milan Kundera's book on the art of the novel.[5]

The elaboration of the literary work begins. When the author accepts the germ of an idea, a progressive game begins between the author and the work. The author cannot do as he or she wishes; the author is conditioned by the work that has been conceived and keeps growing. In the elaboration process, the author does not fully predominate because what is becoming a literary work comes to life and acts on its own. For example, a writer affirms something; and it happens that one of the already written chapters raises objections, asks the author to make that affirmation clear, and demands they adapt it to what is already written. Authors create characters which they shape and depict. They feel the need to respect them; sometimes the power of the character is even so great that it forces the author to submit. It is not unusual to find some author or other narrating some literary experience and revealing that they have sometimes had to 'kill' a character because it had grown so much that it was an obstacle in the original plan (Martín Descalzo in *La frontera de Dios*).[6] Kundera says that what the novelist does is to put the character in a situation, observe it, look at its reactions, and so on.

And so a relationship flows between the work and its author. This influential movement is seen more clearly when the author has to change the beginning or some parts of the text. Miguel Delibes had already written about 100 pages of his *Cinco horas con Mario*, when he discovered that he had to rewrite everything, shifting to a character (the widow) speaking in the first person.[7] His work had acted on the author and carried him further on. During the process of writing the work, the text acts on an author, binding them on one hand and demanding of them on the other. When the work is finished, there are elements that claim to live on. The completed work turns toward the author, as when one character of the plot wants to continue to live; for

5.   Julien Green, *Journal* (Paris: Plon, 1961); Milan Kundera, *The Art of the Novel* (New York: Grove Press, 1980).

6.   Martín Descalzo, *La frontera de Dios* (Barcelona: Planeta, 1956).

7.   Miguel Delibes, *Cinco horas con Mario* (Barcelona: Ediciones Destino, 1969).

example, with John Updike in his four volumes devoted to his character, 'Rabbit'.[8]

In consequence, we have to be conscious of the importance of the text, and the fact that the author is not everything. In some way, the text has made the author.

b. *Movement from the Author to the Receiver*
The author wants to communicate a message that reaches the receiver. This communication is not limited to mere information previously unknown by the reader. It may be the transmission of a live reality, expressed in the text, and which may have multiple facets and forms. The word must have a special quality for this, it must be a rhetorical word, a word that gives language sufficient capacity to delight, persuade, stir—to influence the reader. To influence readers means to change their mentality or to drive them to action. So a complex communication may be produced, and not simply pure information, since, in the rhetorical word, there is an urge to influence the reader and bring into play sentiments, affections, decisions, and so on.

The reader must also accept the reading 'contract' proposed to them by the author. If the writer narrates a fictitious happening, the reader has to accept the tactics used by the author, the reading clue proposed to them, the world in which the work moves and develops. In *Anna Karenina*, Tolstoy creates a poetic world that is the setting in which the action develops, together with the characters and the events. The reader enters this world, a poetical universe created by the author. In a way the author is *making* the reader,[9] the author is modelling them as a reader insofar as he or she invites the reader to share a certain experience, to recreate the universe of a literary work, to come into contact with certain values, sentiments and decisions.[10]

And does the reader act on the author? Let us take the ideal figure of the dialogue where a communicative current is produced which moves to and fro. Outwardly, in the dialogue it seems that there is always

8. J. Updike, *Rabbit Angstrom: A Tetralogy* (London: Everyman's Library, 1995).

9. English-speaking writers use the expression 'to make the reader' more and more frequently.

10. Cf. J.L. Ska, *'Our Fathers Have Told Us': Introduction to the Analysis of Hebrew Narratives* (Analecta Biblica; Rome: Biblical Institute Press, 1990), pp. 42-43.

someone who speaks and another who listens and answers; but this first exterior impression is not sufficient because, to be exact, in the dialogue, the interlocutors alternately occupy the position of the one who speaks and the one who listens; the roles change as the dialogue develops.

The interesting thing is that, in a true dialogue, the listener acts on the speaker, since the speaker, when he begins to speak, mentally takes in the listener. Good speakers take the listener to themself, allow themselves to be influenced by the listener, constitute them as a prospective collaborator in the message to be transmitted. This is the main point: the act of respect for the others inasmuch as they are collaborators, even when my purpose is to convince them of my ideas. An opening is produced in the otherness, in the intersubjectivity of the others; I take into account what is said by the others, who are acting on me, because, when I begin to speak, I am already influenced by what they said previously or by what they expect of me. This attitude transcends the act of listening to oneself, the imperialism of the ego. It has a verbal manifestation in the question we ask the interlocutor in the dialogue so as to know their opinion, their attitude, their information and their needs. On alternatively repeating the mutual acceptance of the interlocutors, the knowledge one has of the other and of oneself is progressively enriched. The otherness changes during the process of the dialogue, the other seems different to me, and I to myself as well.

As can be seen, I am giving a somewhat technical formula for something as well known and elemental as the necessity of keeping the public or the interlocutor in mind when we speak.

In the case we are analysing of the author–receiver relationship, this example of the literal dialogue is not found. If the public, the receiver, is not present, how can it influence the author? It may seem strange to us, but when authors write, they are already taking into account the public, they are accepting the otherness of those to whom they are addressing themselves. 'Say' does not exist, for it is always 'say to'. We have a particular case in the diatribe, which expresses literally that acceptance of the reader by the author. Through this literary figure authors constitute themselves as receiver, in such a way that they develop a dialogue within the discourse they are unfolding. The diatribe is not a fiction in which the author invents an interlocutor; the diatribe expresses the influence of the receiver on the author. Let us look at an example:

- All things are lawful to me.
- Yes, but all things are not expedient. All things are lawful to me but I will not be brought under the power of any.
- Food is for the belly and the belly for food, and besides, God will destroy both.
- But the body is not for fornication but for the Lord, and the Lord for the body. God, who raised the Lord back to life, will also raise us back to life by his power (1 Cor. 6.12-14).

In this example from the first letter to the Corinthians, Paul is not inventing anything new. When he wants to unfold his message, he is conscious that he is addressing himself to others, to subjects he has in his thoughts, to the point of finding it impossible to write without bearing them in mind; so much so that when he is writing his text, they invade his thoughts so forcefully that they stand up and object to Paul in his own literary expression.

This topic of the reader's influence on the author becomes problematic if we think of the future: does the author think of posterity? Perhaps the author does take it into account. Coming to the Bible: did Second Isaiah, who preached hope to his compatriots, think of a Christian community of the second century? How can the twentieth-century reader influence Second Isaiah? This influence cannot exist in a dialogic way. But is it possible to influence the divine author? It is possible from the viewpoint of faith. If we think of the divine author, we are in a context of faith, of the inspired word: the text is there, charged with significance for us. The author did not think of us but the author wrote for us. The book of Jonah ends with a question: to whom is this question addressed? Exclusively to the readers of Jonah after the exile? Not to us?

> The words …were meant to apply not only to Abraham, but to us (Rom. 4.23).

> The scriptures written long ago were all written for our instruction (Rom. 15.4).

> Must not the saying refer to us? (1 Cor. 9.10).

> All those things which happened to them were symbolic, and were recorded as a warning to us (1 Cor. 10.11).

We were already present in God's plan, which is present and reality in the relationship of the author with the listener. If we accept the fact that the Bible is the inspired word, we must see God behind it.

c. *The Movement from the Text to the Receiver*

The movement from the text to the reader is obvious. The text reaches the readers and not only informs them, but communicates meaning to them; the text is an invitation, a dynamic interpellation that reaches the readers.

Can we talk of a dialogical movement between reader and text? The reader feels appealed to by the text, reflects on it and reads it again; the text interpellates them once more, and thus liberates more meaning. This dialogical relationship is produced not only at an individual level, but also at a community level: the human group interpellated by the text has allowed it to mould them, and they then read and understand it again.

It is a fact that there are poor texts that are of no interest, or do not challenge or suggest; but there are also texts that beg a second reading or elicit an answer. Even if the answer is criticism, a confrontation with the text takes place which permits greater penetration into it. We have good grounds for speaking of a pendular alternation between text and reader.

In a way, the reader has power over the text. Readers place themselves and the text in a particular position. I have already indicated this with the example of the contemplation of a painting: we have to look at it from some angle or other. The moment the reader 'frames' the text, perception must necessarily change because the perspective is different. The reader changes the text without touching it, just as the viewer of a painting perceives it differently according to the perspective she or he chooses. The text is not only itself, but is also its relationship with the public.

Since it is communication, the text involves the reader. These two elements may be methodically separated for analysis but they are always related. The correct way of thinking is intersubjective, correlative, one subject that communicates with another. The text cannot be understood if it is isolated.

Summary. There is a complex movement on the author–work–receiver line. There is an alternating flow between the work and the author. When an author elaborates the work they keep the receiver in mind, and the receiver or reader is being shaped when they read the text. A dialogue is also produced between the text and the receiver; the text does not exist alone in itself, but also in relation to the public.

3. *Communication Is not Only Concerned with Information*

When we say that the author communicates their message to the reader, what this message includes must be made clear. We may start from the author, who wants to communicate something or communicate their self; we may pause at the communicating nature of language; we may focus on the contents of the communication. The starting point is secondary; the important thing here is not to confuse communication with information. I consider communication broader and more inclusive than information. There are exegetes who narrow language to the function of communicating ideas and thoughts; they practically reduce it to an enunciative function. But neither the experience of the author nor that crystallized in the text is reduced to ideas, nor is the function of language reduced to enunciation.

Human experience is composed of ideas and sentiments, accompanied by fantasies, moved by desires, enveloped in conceptions, rooted in a subconscious or semiconscious stratum. Language tries to use its resources to communicate this rich and complex experience. Let us focus on the effects.

A prophet may proclaim: 'great is the wrath and anger with which the Lord threatens his people' (Jer. 36.7). Sentiment is thematized, that is, it is converted into the object or subject of a proposition. In such a case, language enunciates the fact of sentiment. But God may say to God's people, 'You do this, and am I going to hold my peace? Do you think I am like you?' (Ps. 50.21). Here wrath is not thematized and enunciated, but rather expressed in the form of questions. The first phrase, 'you do this', more than a statement of fact, is a denunciation, an accusation, a confrontation.

On one occasion, Joshua tries to put the camp in order, because two individuals who have broken out into frenzied manifestations of enraptured prophetism have gone into a spectacular state of ecstasy (Num. 11.26-30). Since he has no authority, he entreats Moses, 'Forbid them to do it'. This is not an enunciation but an imperative, not a command but a petition. However, in this petition, Moses finds a sentiment of Joshua's, not formally expressed but covert and hidden. Joshua has given himself away and Moses has seen through him. 'Are you jealous for me?', that is, 'Can you not tolerate my losing an exclusive right or monopoly?'

Exegetes must be like Moses: they listen not only to the doctrine enunciated by Paul on sin, but also to the passion with which it is pronounced (Rom. 7). The enthusiasm with which he sings of love is part of his message (1 Cor. 13). Exegetes frequently pay these aspects little attention. It is up to hermeneutical reflection to bring them to the surface and integrate them into its system.

The poetic text happily succeeds in capturing vibrant human experience and communicates it with its privileged language.

No less important is interpellation as a component of total communication. This also may be thematized, in imperatives, optatives, exclamations or apostrophes: 'Listen, heavens, hear me, earth' (is this an address to the created universe or to human listeners?); 'If only my people would listen to me!' (Ps. 81.14); 'You are that man!' (2 Sam. 12.7); 'Those men have started to think of their idols... Am I going to allow them to consult me?' (Ezek. 14.4); 'Woe betide those heroic topers, those valiant mixers of drink' (Isa. 5.22).

There are many ways of interpellating. In the song to the vineyard (Isa. 5.1-7) we witness the leap from lyric (expression) to rhetoric (interpellation). Practically all prophetic activity comes into this sphere: but in a confessional context, that is, for whoever receives the Bible as the Word of God, the whole Bible unfolds its power of interpellation in a diversity of ways. Narrative texts also do so, sometimes more forcefully. Even nature itself, or the harmony of the temple become denunciations and calls to humans (Ps. 104; Ezek. 43.10-11). Bultmann affirmed and proclaimed this with paradoxical exaggeration, claiming that interpellation was the only valid communication of the Bible. Of course, there were also exegetes who preferred to converse and discuss with Bultmann rather than allow themselves to be interpellated by the Bible. With their words they said he was right, but with their activity as interpreters, they rejected his theory. If we focus on language as the mediator of communication, the above squares with the theory of the functions of language.[11]

4. *The Dialogical Structure of Comprehension*

At a philosophical and literary level, H.G. Gadamer's analysis shows the dialogical character of comprehension.[12] When we want to under-

---

11. Cf. Alonso Schökel, *The Inspired Word*, pp. 134-50.
12. H.G. Gadamer, *Truth and Method* (New York: Seabury, 1975).

stand a literary work, the text (which is presented as a complete structure), opens itself in the reading stage to a kind of dialogue between two interlocutors. The reader is invited or challenged to contribute with questions, answers and reactions so that the maximum communication may be produced. We should not content ourselves with Plato's disenchanted diagnosis (*Phaedrus* 58) of the written text, which he compares to a silent painting in front of him, as it does not answer, it gives no explanation, it does not defend itself, and it does not address itself to people concerned. Plato is partly right, but the restive searching reader makes a text speak and answer. The active reader will never describe a text depicting it as the psalmists depicted the idols:

> They have mouths and do not speak, they have eyes and do not see,
> they have ears and do not hear, they have noses and do not smell,
> they have hands and do not touch, they have feet and do not walk,
> they have no voice in their throats (Ps. 115.5-7).

Faced with these verses of Quevedo (1580–1645) dedicated to the paintbrush, 'Al pincel', all we can say is that the text really and truly speaks to the reader:

> Pomp, price and beauty are yours;
> you reform death's envy
> and ingeniously restitute
> what it so cruelly effaces ...
>
> Thanks to you and your coordination
> the living communicate with the dead;
>
> Thanks to you the brief present
> which as yet barely sees the back of the past,
> the past which flees wrested from life,
> communicates with it and deals with it face to face.
>
> Who in all places
> are, simply by looking, dwellers.

How can we engage in a dialogue with a text? Is it possible to place it in a dialogic situation? St Augustine said that a text closes so that we have to knock and make it open. It is positively closed because it wants us to knock.

We always tackle a text with precisely framed questions or simply with curiosity and a global, generic approach. Two attitudes may be discerned. The first poses the question to the text with rigour and precision. As a reader I accept various answers; I do not prejudge them, I do not seek confirmation of what I know or expect; I do not have the answer ready. But the question has centred, guided and conditioned the answer of the text. The second attitude offers the question, but is prepared for the text to restate the question, to denounce my approach, to transfer me to another problem. I ask and the text says, 'that is not the point', 'the real problem is this other one', 'you must look in that direction...'

In Mk 12.18-27, the Sadducees pose a casuistic problem to Jesus in relation with the law of levirate marriage. They do not believe in the resurrection; that is their hard-and-fast immovable posture. The question is posed only to strengthen themselves in their own beliefs. Jesus's answer is not directly addressed to the case in question: 'How far you are from the truth! You know neither the scriptures nor the power of God.' With this he denounces their posture, places them in another sphere and moves them to a different situation which was hidden from them by their unquestioned prejudices.

The same thing happens in the dialogue between Jesus and the Pharisees and followers of Herod on the tribute to Caesar (Mk 12.13-17). Jesus changes the case of his interlocutors. It is not a case of whether the tribute must be paid or not, but of giving God God's image, which is human.

A similar case is narrated in ch. 7 of the book of Zechariah, where there is a liturgical consultation which receives an ethical answer. The claimants were in a false position; it was not ritual questions they had to settle, but rather justice in social relations.

A similar thing occurs in dialogue with the text. If I seek an answer to my questions in the text, it will very possibly reply with another series of questions and ask me to pose my enquiries in a different way. The text leads to dialogue.

When we read a text, we do so starting from our interests and preoccupations. I place myself in relation to the text and place the text in a correspondent relation to me. The text speaks to me according to that mutual position, and it will very possibly provoke me, producing in me a restlessness that will impel me to read again. The subsequent contact with the text will be different from the first. My position as reader has changed: the adaptation to the situation for which the text was calling has come about.

Let us take Psalm 82. If we leave aside the identification of the characters, it is a relatively easy poem to understand. We may briefly summarize the original idea of the psalm: There are many divinities who are charged by the supreme God to watch over justice among people. The supreme God, Yahweh, calls them to report to God, and when they show that they have failed in their mission, God condemns them to death and takes over universal government.

Let us read the psalm with our problems, convictions and conceptions as modern Christians. The positive part of Psalm 82, the Lord's image as defender of the rights of the oppressed, is easy to comprehend and assimilate. Far from easy is the vivid reference to other divinities, so alien to our horizon. Does the biblical author really believe that other gods existed, and that they were not immortal? In what sense is it said that they judged and governed humanity until the Lord took charge?

Faced with these questions, one's reaction may be of rejection, dispensing with this psalm as a useless archaeological piece, full of primitive beliefs devoid of contemporary significance. This attitude would mean violently imposing our horizon on the psalm and denying its original meaning.

However, if we apply a dialogical process, making the issues of the text engage in a dialogue with those of other biblical authors and with ours—for example: mortality and nullity in Second Isaiah (i.e. if they are mortal, are they gods?); gods and justice; God's justice and human injustice; idols' mental lifelessness, and so on—the result of this process of interpretation will be different. We will succeed in bringing to light the profound meaning of the psalm which is latent and potential in its symbolical expression.

In the dialogue with the text, we perceive that the many gods were human efforts to express the religious experience of many peoples. This expression is conditioned by the human, social and historical experience of each individual people. As for particular symbolic representations of what is divine, they correspond, in a way, to divine reality. The affirmation that unjust conduct radically falsifies a representation of divinity is a most important religious intuition, which is not only pragmatic, but also metaphysical. The psalm puts us on guard before erroneous conceptions of God and their consequences in social relations.

We must avow that we would not have reached this comprehension if we had not struck up a dialogue with the psalm. We would not have advanced if we had dispensed with the psalm as a superceded relic. We have, rather, practised a dialectic reflection which has led us to the fusion or adjustment of the horizons of the psalm and ours. The text has succeeded in disclosing the vast profundity of its vision to us.

5. *Pre-comprehension*

According to the ideals of author-hermeneutics, the reader must discard everything that comes between the reader and objectivity; but we have seen that, contrary to this, the reader does belong to the overall process of comprehension. There are two correlate elements: the text in relation with the reader and the reader herself or himself, who harbours several factors previous to the act of comprehension.

Knowledge of something and previous interest in: These are expressions which clearly indicate the position of the reader previous to the interpretative act. This goes against the ideal of the reader's neutrality, but is based on the reality of experience. When the reader begins to read, there exists a previous relationship of interest. The reader does not come to the text as a neutral subject approaching an inert object. The text is not simply text, but rather text towards the reader. They are *two* poles in the dialogue which develops comprehension.

We call *pre-comprehension* the knowledge the reader has of the topic before reading the text. Degrees may be accepted in such knowledge, although in some cases a relative threshold must be surmounted. Pre-comprehension has been obtained via channels different from the work to be read—via immediate personal experience, via the information given by others. Pre-comprehension may coincide with a partial horizon.

Once that reading and comprehension of the work are finished, the process may be repeated at a higher level. What I know after having read and understood the book is converted into the pre-comprehension of a second reading or an analytical study. This process may be repeated according to the richness of the text in question and the personal capacity of the reader. Without the radical capacity of the reader, and a relative threshold of knowledge, comprehension is impossible—not everyone is capable of understanding a book of metaphysics, not even after repeated efforts!

The last consideration leads us to the examination of another aspect. Although it will always be intellectual, pre-comprehension may be inscribed in the sphere of responsible action. If the text is charged with demands, if it calls for arduous action, then it requires a basic attitude of response from the readers/listeners. They may understand the sense very well and refuse to respond, but it could also happen that previous resistance prevents authentic comprehension. The principle is understood on the intellectual level, but its demands are not grasped. Analogously, we could call the required previous attitude pre-comprehension. Perhaps it would be more appropiate to call it predisposition. When God sends Ezekiel the prophet, He says to him:

> Son of Adam, go, go forth to the House of Israel and tell them my words, for you are not being sent to a people of strange language and foreign tongues which you do not understand. Should I send you to these, they would certainly pay heed to you. On the contrary, the House of Israel will not pay heed to you because they will not pay heed to me (Ezek. 3.4-7).

For those obstinate hearers, it is as if Ezekiel's message were given in an unintelligible foreign language. They do not understand because they do not want to understand. There is none so deaf as one who will not hear, a theme which John's Gospel repeats tirelessly. As such, it is better not to restrict the scope of his texts to the Jewish authorities, thought to be the first hearers; this would deprive the text of its force of appeal for us. To restrict it is to invalidate the comprehension of the message.

On the contrary, there are readers of the gospel who devote their lives to self-denying charity, and understand the evangelical message with exceptional clarity and profundity, because they possess a predisposition which favours direct comprehension. Let us take the case of the Good Samaritan; those who are used to the constant exercise of charity know who the neighbour is, and so profoundly understand the gospel story, because their lifestyle predisposes them to it.

The comprehension of the sense is a complex activity that may implicate the whole person. The reader does not practise a systematic inhibition of all that is not pure intellect when confronting the biblical text. The teacher may take refuge in a limited intellectual field, leaving the rest aside. But this specialized understanding is not the universal model of comprehension. Hermeneutics has to observe the phenomenon in all its amplitude.

Apocalyptic and eschatological writers sometimes appeal to the perspicacity of the reader. They slip in references indicating that they are writing in code. Is knowledge of the code in Daniel, the Apocalypse or

some gospel discourses a form of comprehension? It is rather a question of language; the code is a language within a language. We sometimes find texts with a cue—a good example of this is Mark's apocalyptic discourse:

> 'When you see the abomination of desolation usurping a place which is
> not his (let the reader understand ...)' (Mk 13.14).

In the book of Revelation we have another example. At the end of ch.
13, the author clearly says that he has spoken in code:

> This calls for skill: Let anyone who has understanding decipher the
> number of the beast, for it is the number of a man. And the number is
> 666 (Rev. 13.18).

A certain degree of sensitivity is necessary in order to understand.
This means an attitude that does not require an 'objective neutrality'
nor 'self-effacement' on the part of the readers, but rather that they
should become aware of their own precomprehension and predisposition. It is essential to be conscious of this so that the text may be
present in its otherness. Its truth will appear when the text confronts the
interpreter.

6. *The Hermeneutical Circle*

The work–receiver movement gives us a motive for treating the appar-
ent paradox of human understanding activity which has its logical
application in the interpretative act. This paradox arises from the relationship established between the totality and the part, between what is
generic and what is particular. We have said that the reader enters the
text with a personal reality. The reader's world and horizon condition a
particular comprehension of a specific text; and the text in turn broad-
ens the reader's total horizon. Curiously, not only may what is singular
be understood starting from the whole, but also the whole may be
understood starting from what is singular. In hermeneutical reflection,
this way of functioning is alluded to with the denomination *hermeneutical circle*. It was Heidegger who demonstrated this fundamental
circular structure of human understanding. Gadamer picked up Heidegger's concepts, made them fructify, and has gathered them together
in detail,[13] and E. Coreth has also dealt with the problem of the herme-

13. Cf. H.G. Gadamer, *Truth and Method* (London: Sheed & Ward, 2nd edn,
1989).

neutical circle in his hermeneutical theory.[14] I develop this theme following, fundamentally, these last two authors.

The term *hermeneutical circle* has become unavoidably integrated into modern hermeneutics. The fact that it lends itself to misuse is no reason to banish it, for the structure designated by this formula governs various relationships of the complex theorems of comprehension and explanation. By hermeneutical circle, we understand the correlativity of two factors and their mutual conditioning in the act of understanding and explaining. When two people converse to understand each other, the word passes from one to the other, the roles of I and You change, continually returning to a preceding point. This return may suggest the image of the circle in the same way that the alternating movement of a connecting rod may generate the circular movement of a wheel. To others it may suggest rather the image of a pendulum or swing, in which the point of arrival is alternately conditioned by the point of departure; which, by impulses, may open or close the arc of oscillation and which draws a semicircular figure.

In the dialogue supposed between the text and reader, not everything is reduced to grammatical changes of subject and object, but rather an interchange from one to the other is mentally produced. An area of meaning is shared in order to accept it, reject it or make progress. This mental communication, mediated by the word, may also be imagined as a circular or pendular movement.

Now let us imagine a thinker immersed in a theme or problem. They may have had an instantaneous intuition as to its meaning; other times they have to think the matter over—returning to it time and again and finding the way to grasp and explain the solution to themselves. Even when the thinker starts off from intuition, they have to rotate and articulate it. Long ago, the writer of Ecclesiastes had already used the expression 'to turn things over in one's mind'. Something similar happens to the literary critic or to anyone who analyses a text—one has to 'return' to it, has to 'think it over'; has to 'make it rotate' before an inquisitive gaze.

Can or should we say that the hermeneutic circle is a vicious circle? By no means. The vicious circle is a logical operation that consists in presupposing the conclusion in the premises, or in taking for granted

14. Cf. E. Coreth, *Grundfragen der Hermeneutik: Ein philosophischer Beitrag* (Freiburg: Herder, 1969), pp. 107-117.

what is being demonstrated. It is a relative of 'begging the question'. The hermeneutical circle presupposes something, but does not take it for granted. It does not withdraw into itself; on the contrary, it opens itself to correction and enrichment. Due to its progressive character, some would prefer to call it the 'hermeneutical spiral'; because, as it rotates, it extends its range, embracing more, or specifying and perfecting what has been previously embraced. But because Schleiermacher had already spoken of circumference and circle, the term is now acclimatized and refuses to be substituted for another, more exact term.[15]

A preliminary description will situate the hermeneutical circle in correlation with the whole and the part, with what is general and what is particular: we understand the part according to the whole and the whole according to the parts; we understand what is general starting from the particular and the particular when referred to what is general.

The whole and the part are easy to observe in a typical sentence. Let us consider the following:

> Put your best foot forward.
> A project is afoot to build a new motorway.
> She waits on him hand and foot.
> George is very tall—he's six foot three.

I understand the meaning of each sentence by an organic synthesis of its components: I understand 'foot', 'on foot', and the others, according to the complete sentence. In the long grammatical periods of Latin rhetoric and in modern German, the meaning is kept back until the last word or the last verbal component—'aus, zu, vor, an...'—is pronounced. The mind anticipates a global intellection that is progressively corrected, or carries out partial comprehension that is gradually completed.

Another significant, though formal, example is the perception of a melody. I need to hear all the notes to the end of the musical phrase so as to capture the melody; but each note makes sense in the whole phrase for its relationships of interval, duration and intensity, depending on the key. As if this were not enough, relationships of harmony, counterpoint and timbre are frequently added to the melodic ones.[16]

---

15. Cf. R.E. Palmer, *Hermeneutics: Interpretation Theory in Schleiermacher, Dilthey, Heidegger and Gadamer* (Evanston, IL: Northwestern University Press, 1969).

16. Composers sometimes state the key at the beginning, for example, the A minor chord which opens Beethoven's 7th symphony. At other times they play at

The totality may be the text, for example, a sonnet. If it is well wrought, its plenitude of meaning and the sense of each verse are unveiled only with the last verse. The totality may also be the text and its life or literary context (e.g. a sonnet within a classic drama), whose situation makes the text clear. Note the ambiguity in 'Did you catch that?'—depending on the situation, I could be referring to a ball or an allusion.

Anyone who sets about interpreting a text sets a project in motion.[17] On the basis of the immediate meaning given by the text, the reader first outlines the meaning of the whole. Comprehension consists in the elaboration of this preliminary project, which is continually revised from the result of the reader's ensuing grasp of the text. All revision of the initial project brings with it the possibility of outlining a new project of meaning. This means that contrasted projects may be interlaced in an elaboration that, in the end, brings a clearer vision of the unity of the meaning. It also means that comprehension may begin with provisional concepts that are gradually substituted for others that are more appropriate.

What is general may be considered as a set made up of individualities. This time I give a biblical example, a literary genre. In order to define a literary genre, I must first gather the relevant individualities in order to discover and define their consistant features. In order to unite the individualities I must know the genre so as to apply certain criteria of identification. The operation would be impossible if an alternative process of project and verification were not carried out.

Schleiermacher spoke of two ways or methods of understanding the individual; by divination, when, in a way, one is transformed into the other in order to immediately understand what is individual; and, by comparison, when one proposes the object first as generic and then tries to understand what is particular by comparison with other individuals

---

misleading us. For instance, in the same composer's 4th concerto for piano and orchestra, the piano states a thematic phrase in G major, and immediately afterwards, the orchestra surprises us with the phrase in B major. I have to listen to its evolution so as to see the function it has. Formal music gives a remarkable demonstration of the play of relationships and functions and the correlative structure of the whole and its parts.

17. Cf. Palmer, *Hermeneutics*, pp. 224-35: on the collocation of the text in a dialogical situation.

of the same type. The two methods are mutually involved and are correlative in their application.

A qualitative step is taken when we consider that the subject enters the circle and is a part of the whole process. If for 'sense' we understand 'what is intelligible in a being', people grasp the sense of a being X as Z—as a book, as a gift, as weight, as a task. That 'understanding as' constitutes the being in an object of knowledge and supposes a point of view. This point of view is provided and conditioned by the repertoire of knowledge which the subject has.

In a way, the intelligible object is constituted by the subject when the subject contemplates it from the subject's point of view. Having the evidence being before one does not yet mean understanding it. This sense perceived as 'understanding as' is articulated later in the proposition and the explanation.

Now, the point of view is conditioned by my present repertory of knowledge, and this is conditioned by the place I occupy in history. When I want to know a historical fact or text, I cannot step outside history in order to observe it because I am part of a history which has been influenced or conditioned by that fact or text. (Positivism in its diverse forms considers the sense of a text perfectly and definitely constituted by the conscious decision of the author; and it assumes the subject to be outside history and not conditioned by it.) The Bible is a special case of this human structure of knowledge, with a factor that transcends the mere human process. As an ancient human text, it is submitted to the universal structure of human comprehension and explanation, but, due to its character which we denominate *inspired*, the Bible achieves that structure at other levels. Faith comes by hearing the word of the gospel (Rom. 10.17), but the word may be received as 'Gospel' only with faith. The inspired Word is the bearer of the Spirit, but in order to receive it as inspired I must possess the Spirit. I come to the theme of the Scripture by the word, but on considering the theme I criticize that word. In addition, the historical influence of that word has been particularly intense, so that the believer is deeply conditioned by that word and its later history when she or he comes to comprehend it. In other words, how does the first entrance into the world of salvation come about? By the word. But if I do not know what it tells me, I cannot understand it; if I understand it, I am already inside.

A radical human opening to salvation must be taken as a total horizon: on this horizon comes the call of God, expressed in words or not, which claims the response of faith. That word or call holds, as a constitutive factor, the Spirit who will act with humankind in the act of receiving and responding. Moreover, access to the experience of faith is not exclusive to Scripture. By other individual or social ways I may attain a spiritual experience homogenous with the experience expressed by the biblical text, which allows me to comprehend it.

This is the human way of understanding; it is no imaginary construct. When we are interpreting a text, we are carrying out an intersubjective action. There is circularity between text and reader. As interpreter-reader I am part of that circularity.

Summary. Communication is not only information. It is possible and necessary to engage in a dialogue with the text. For this, it is worth having an opening towards the text, in the form of pre-comprehension and predisposition. In the comprehension of the literary work the reader is part of the process, a circular process where the part is understood by the whole and the whole by the part.

Chapter 6

THE AUTHOR–THEME–RECEIVER LINE

When we speak of pre-comprehension, the hermeneutical circle, the dialogical structure of understanding, the factor of the theme or topic included in communication arises.

Frequently, on reading a text, listening to a speech or participating in a conversation we hear the expression, 'I don't know what he's talking about', which we may understand in two ways. First, I understand what he says, but I do not know to whom or what he is referring—a problem of identification. This is a common scene in the Gospels: Mk 4.3-13, where the disciples do not understand the parable of the sower; or Mt. 21.33-46, the parable of the vineyard and the labourers, where the high priests and the Pharisees really did 'realize that it was aimed at them'. Secondly, I do not understand the theme being talked about, and that is why I do not understand what is being said—a problem of ignorance. When the theme is unfamiliar, the words lose their context and lose their meaning for the listener.

In communication, the individual message springs from a plurality and is based on multiple links with it, explicit or not. We understand the message by accepting it in a plurality, discovering and creating links. We call this complex plurality 'horizon'.[1]

1. The Horizon as a Cognitive Element

Aristotle and scholasticism strove to comprehend the act of intellectual knowledge, which they considered as an isolated individual act, but comprehension absolutely isolated from a context of contents does not exist. This is a theme that emerges continually in modern philosophy,

1.   For the exposition of this theme, we are going to follow basically the approach offered by Coreth, *Grundfragen der Hermeneutik*, pp. 95-106.

although under diverse aspects. From a metaphysical point of view, it underlies the distinction between appropriate and inappropriate ideas, typical of Spinoza and Leibniz. In Hegel, it acquires a systematic development, and in historical knowledge and the science of the spirit, the concept that what is singular has to be understood in a wider context is a contribution of Scheiermacher and Droysen, who influence Dilthey.

In Husserl, the problems are amplified beyond psychological and historical comprehension to general phenomenological signification. It is Husserl who introduces the concept of a horizon: the totality of what is athematically seen or anticipated in systematic singular knowledge. Thus a horizon structure is characteristic of all experience, since it is accompanied by previous knowledge of contents or purposes which have not reached the fact on which the act of comprehension is carried out. Husserl's theory is then developed by Heidegger in his attempt to elucidate the phenomenon of the 'totality of nature' in the context of 'being in the world'.

The same problem arises again from the philosophy of language. In contrast with the repeated attempts of the neo-positivists to understand language atomically, there is a growing belief that a word does not have a unanimously determined signification before its verbal use, but that the signification is established in the live occurrences in daily language. Furthermore, the context of action or signification from which the significance of a word or an affirmation is determined alludes beyond itself to the live totality of human understanding and speech.

In today's hermeneutical reflection, the horizon concept is fundamental, Coreth describes it thus:

> A totality comprehended or grasped in a non-thematized manner which enters the knowledge of an individual content, conditioning and determining it, so that this content is manifested in a specific way within the totality.[2]

Every act of understanding individual content, whether it is an object or a fact or a text, is a grasping of 'sense', and the sense is manifested in a context or relationship of sense. That context of sense both makes possible and conditions the new comprehension of sense.

Think of a pocket calculator shown to people of a primitive tribe: they will perceive it without understanding it, and we cannot explain

---

2. Coreth, *Grundfragen der Hermeneutik*, p. 104.

the 'sense' of it to them, because they lack the knowledge of the elements to be referred to and in which to inscribe their perception. We recognize the instrument because we immediately inscribe or refer to the complex of our knowledge of mechanics, electronics, handling, functions and mathematical operations. It is clear that previous knowledge may be very varied, from the elemental kind of our civilization to that of a specialist in the area, and this previous knowledge conditions and determines specific comprehension, forming part of it. This influence on comprehension is not developed in an explicit, enunciated way each time, but as a tacit presupposed foundation, that is, in a non-thematic way. It is a non-thematized complex in the act of new comprehension.

What we say about an object or a fact also goes for a text, whether literary, philosophical or scientific. It presupposes previous knowledge of a linguistic universe as a 'language' (*langue*) accumulated in many experiences of 'words' (*parole*). This linguistic universe does not enter individual comprehension in a thematized manner: this would be an unbearable burden and confusing multiplicity. The aforesaid can be applied to a language, for example, Spanish, German, Chinese, or a specific language, for example, philosophical, poetic or political.

The horizon may be *total* or *partial*. The total horizon is the entirety of our personal or transmitted human experience. The partial horizon may have diverse dimensions and aspects. It may refer to practical action or theoretical sense as complementary moments, to a particular discipline, or to a sphere of human activity.

But every horizon of sense, even narrow and limited, whether theoretical or practical, in which the individual act of knowledge happens, refers to the totality of sense of our existence. The partial horizon is always referred to the total horizon: all I have experienced, seen, read, studied; the totality of being, to which I am open as an intelligent creature. It is not so much the totality of 'what I know' as 'what I am' that is athematically present in every individual act of understanding.

When we speak of horizon we do not refer only to something theoretical. What we might call a practical horizon of skill, knowing 'how to do something', also comes into play. This is the practical horizon of living, the experimental field of common sense, of wisdom (the biblical *hokma*). Sheet music is read differently by a person who can play the piano than by a teacher of solfeggio who cannot. This has important consequences for the Christian reading of the Bible. Christian life constitutes the horizon of genuine comprehension of evangelical, Pauline or Old Testament language.

The horizon is related to experience; not to individual experience, but to experience/common sense/expertise accumulated in a global manner. It is not objectifiable knowledge, instead, it conditions and determines new individual experiences. This overall experience is progressive, temporal and historical.

The horizon *grows*, and widens with each new experience and piece of acquired knowledge. Just as, while climbing a mountain, we have an increasingly widening view of the horizon widening before us, so do new elements enter this horizon, and each fact is affected by the new context. Thanks to its ability to grow, the horizon gives us the possibility of an increasing comprehension of a person or a text.

A person: every instance of contact or observation, every moment of communication and dialogue brings new knowledge of the other, widening my horizon, and determining and improving each successive act of communication. Each new piece of information is added to, organically hooked on to the complex of accumulated preceding knowledge which produces my global knowledge.

Similarly, there is the case of the text which, thanks to this mechanism, may enter a dialogical situation. The first reading occurs within my constituted horizon. Up to a certain point I understand the text, and with it I acquire new knowledge that now forms part of a widened horizon. With it I begin the second reading, which is no longer the same as the first. And so on until the sense of the text has been thoroughly, or according to my capacity, transmitted.

From this perspective of the growing horizon, we may say that a text is always new, since the horizon of the reader is different and wider every day. Each time the individual acquires new knowledge, the horizon is enriched, and the enriched horizon makes it possible to know the text better.

We must add another factor to the growth of the horizon. This is correction: the capacity of the object, the fact, the text I know, to correct me, make me revise, reflect, bring up enigmas and questions. Each day, each new piece of knowledge, each experience widens and amplifies the horizon, or revises and corrects it. The stimulus is curiosity—the true symptom of youth.

Another characteristic of the horizon is its *immediacy-mediation*. If the horizon is a 'condition of possibility', in a way it is a mediator of individual knowledge. But as the horizon does not act in a thematized way, individual knowledge occurs immediately as sudden instantaneous enlightenment. Reciprocally, the horizon is the result of acquired or incorporated multiple experiences or knowledge which prove to be its mediators: therefore, it is mediate. But with respect to the condition of possibility, it is immediate. It is the relationship between condition and mediation, totality and individual, the whole and a part.

The *components* of the horizon are *heterogenous*. For example, in literature I may be more interested in the lyric than the narrative or the drama. In consequence, my sensibility is greater for capturing what is lyric; my literary knowledge is not homogeneous, regular and compact. For this reason, the influence of the horizon and its components on a text or the reader's comprehension is also heterogeneous. Furthermore, the author's horizon and that of the reader are also heterogenous.

According to Gadamer's theory, the horizons of the author and the reader come into contact in the comprehension of the text. In the reader–text dialogue, a fusion of the two horizons is sought. In the reading, the gradual fusion of the two horizons is essential so as to reach a common horizon.

However, Coreth considers that a fusion that totally identifies the two horizons is impossible. He proposes that an approximation or an adjustment of horizons must be acheived. The reader will try to approach the author's horizon, but always conserving their own; which, by its necessary law of growth, changes when engaging in a dialogue with a different horizon from theirs, such as the author's.

Without meaning to, St Augustine gives us a profound lesson of hermeneutics on the fusion of horizons:

> We frequently get bored repeating the same thing when relating to children. Let us try to tune in with them with fraternal, paternal or maternal love and on joining our hearts with theirs, that thing will seem new to us. So powerful is the harmony of affection that, when they receive the action of our words and we receive the reaction of their apprenticeship, we take up abode within each other. It is as if they said in us what they hear, and as if we learned from them what we teach. Does not the same thing happen with vast beautiful landscapes of towns or the countryside? We are so used to seeing them that we pass them by without enjoying them. We show them to others who have not seen them before and when they enjoy what is a novelty for them, our enjoyment is also renewed. The greater the friendship between us, the greater is our pleasure, because on our being in them thanks to the bond of love, all that was old becomes new.

However, if we have made progress in the contemplation of human beings, it does not suffice us that our friends are happy and are marvelled to observe human works. Rather, we wish to raise them towards the plan and skill of he who produced them, so that they soar to admire and praise God, Creator of all things, ultimate fruitful objective of love. So much greater should be our delight when men draw near to learn God himself, for whom we have to learn all that is to be learnt. With their novelty we must renew ourselves, and if our accustomed predication grows cold, may their unaccustomed attention imbue it with new warmth.

Something else will increase our joy: thinking and considering how man passes from the death of error to the life of faith. With what beneficent pleasure do we traverse familiar streets when we direct someone who is lost: then with greater promptness and delight should we travel the paths we need not repeat so as to lead the confused hapless soul along the path of peace. We have been commanded thus by he who conceded it to us.[3]

In this text, we first observe the correlativity of two subjects in the process: the interpreter and the listener. Then comes a kind of 'horizon adjustment', in which affection (often forgotten by modern experts) participates as a decisive factor. Discovery is helped when we interpret for others. Finally, we find the ascending movement: from the work to expertise (the faculty of execution), from this to the author's project (not pure ideas), from there to the author himself, the reason for the knowledge and the ultimate object of love.

Summary. By definition, the horizon is athematic, growing, heterogenous in its composition, with theoretical and practical elements accumulated. In consequence, it is unequal in its conditioning influence on each act of comprehension; because of its character of mediacy–immediacy.

2. The Question

The question thematizes the horizon. As we have said, the horizon is athematic, but may gradually, partially, be thematized. One especially good way of doing this is the question.

a. The Question Thematizes the Horizon
A text is an answer to a question authors have asked themselves, thematizing their horizon. For this reason, 'he who wants to comprehend a

3.   St Augustine, *De catechizandis rudibus* 1.12.17.

text must retreat with his questions further back than what has been said; he has to understand it as the answer to a question whose answer is the text. Drawing back thus beyond what has been said the reader reaches even further back to its origin. A text is understood only when the horizon of questioning has been reached'.[4] On asking the question, the entity is unveiled, and has given itself away. I have forced that potential being that is there but had not shown itself. The being is there, I force it with my question and it reveals itself. The being is made evident by the one who asked the question. The being is concealed, shut in its safe; I force the lock with my question and the being is revealed.

Furthermore, authors not only pose questions, but also define them. They establish what scholastics call *status quaestionis*, a dialectical recourse that consists in defining the question, 'What is under discussion here?'—an invention or recourse of great value that has not lost interest.

Readers also have particular horizons where they live. It is the moment that arrives when I myself pose a question and define it; I thematize a point on my horizon, favouring it, placing it in the foreground, and thus giving it the power of relevance.

b. *Dynamics of the Question*

The question consists in knowing that we do not know. It is in itself a negativity (no-knowledge) that is born and lives only in positivity (knowledge). In order to formulate a question, it is essential to know something about the theme, and at the same time to know that one does not know. For example, one who knows nothing about the Bible does not know their ignorance. Conscious ignorance is found only in the context of knowledge. The question is thus defined as the consciousness of no-knowledge in the sphere of knowledge (the Socratic *docta ignorantia*).

c. *The Question in the History of Biblical Hermeneutics*

For a long time in the Middle Ages, the Bible was interpreted *per sensus*: the literal and spiritual meaning. On the literal sense of the texts (history) was superimposed a spiritual sense, which in turn was produced in three steps in this order: allegory, tropology, anagoge, following the distich

---

4.   Gadamer, *Truth and Method* (1975), p. 448.

Littera gesta docet, quid credas allegoria,
moralis quid agas, quod tendas anagogia.[5]

At a certain point, the mediaeval authors started to make exegesis *per quaestiones*: casting specific questions at the biblical text, questions of moral, spiritual, dogmatic and other types; questions that may later be organized and systematized.

That moment, which is the historical key to the advance from interpretation *per sensus* to *per quaestiones*, illuminates this exposition. Interpretation *per sensus* was already a way of asking. *Per quaestiones* involves a transposition, a change of key. The way of asking determines the way of interpreting, since the question thematizes the horizon and orientates the answer.

Let us not forget that the text also poses its questions to the reader, and may correct the reader's questions, thus establishing a dialogue. The text may give rise to questions in its dialogical functioning, it may correct, or even substitute questions.

d. *The Primacy of the Question*

It is essential for a question to have sense. Sense means direction. The sense of the question is the direction in which the answer can be found if it is to be a sensible and meaningful answer. The question acts on its object by placing it in a specific perspective. The raising of a question forces its object to come to being. The *logos* displayed by this forcibly opened being is now, in this sense, always an answer.

The Socrates presented to us by Plato makes this great contribution: it is more difficult to ask than to answer. In the quasi-comic interchange of questions and answers, of knowledge and no-knowledge, it may be recognized that, for all knowledge and discourse that wants to know the sense of things, the question comes first.

In interpretation, it is vital to know what we are asking the text. We have no doubts in recognizing the importance of an exegetical method, but we must not forget that a previous question underlies each method, a question that is more serious than the method itself, since this latter is directed by the former.

---

5.   For a deeper study of the senses of the Scriptures according to mediaeval reflection, cf. L. Alonso Schökel, *Hermeneútica de la palabra*, I (Madrid: Cristiandad, 1986), pp. 69-72.

Questions may be theoretical, speculative or practical. A vital horizon of intensive and active Christian life produces vital questions. A speculative laboratory horizon gives rise to speculative questions. A rich horizon may provide multiple and varied questions. In this sense, it is not a bad idea to take into account the signs of the times, the events that it is our lot to live.

It is absolutely non-scientific to postulate that science is not made by those who ask vital questions. As if, in order to be scientists, it were necessary to dispense with life in the interests of objectivity and precision! The richer the horizon of the person, the more ample will be the spectrum of questions. The richness of a person who interprets a text (the exegete), lies in the plurality, quality and variety of the questions formulated to the text.

Summary. The question thematizes the horizon by developing its dynamics of knowledge/no-knowledge. The question acts on its object and places it in a specific perspective. Because of this, it is in our interest to know what we ask a text and of what type are our questions.

e. *The Provisional Character of Hermeneutics*
On the horizon of the question, Gadamer observes some negative aspects which are not, in my opinion, so negative:

–   Up to a point, what is discovered corrects what goes before. Because of this, it is necessary to have the humility to understand and the disposition to humble oneself before the discovery of a new comprehension.
–   However, what has been discovered also enriches.
–   Expectations are sometimes frustrated; we find less than we expected.
–   However, sometimes expectations fall short because discovery has exceeded them.
–   Constant correction demonstrates our finiteness to us. Humanity gradually becomes conscious of its limitations and, as it learns, doubts itself more and more.
–   However, each act of comprehension always opens a new experience to us.

3. *Notes on Imagination*

On the line of the Author–Theme–Receiver relationship that we are analysing, one aspect that appears in the relationship between the three factors emerges forcefully: imagination.

Artists, narrators or poets use imagination in various forms. They invent plots and characters. They imagine a scene: a house, room, wood, path. They look at it from without as a spectators, or move to the interior and participate. In his visions, Ezekiel is not a simple spectator—he acts, even as the leading character. In the scene of the dry bones (Ezek. 37.1-14), he has to pronounce the incantation, and then contemplate its effects. In the scene of the spring in the temple (Ezek. 47.1-5), he has to cross the water three times and feel it on his skin. It is as when we dream; we are not mere spectators.

When authors create their characters, in a way they have to get inside them, observe or share their feelings. They have to put themselves in the characters' place, at the same time observing how they act and react. The author confronts Judith with Holofernes. The author is neither a beautiful woman nor a proud general, but in fantasy is both, and is also the one who observes how the meeting develops (the musician also creates a melody to which he himself listens inwardly). Afterwards, in the execution, when authors write their tales or poems, they resort to other alternatives of the imagination: descriptive details, metaphors and symbols. Judith reclines on a fleece while she eats with Holofernes; another touch of sensuality (cf. Jud. 12.10-20).

At this stage, an author should not describe everything; they do not need to. Their art consists in selecting the details that re-create the whole scene. The hands of the woman on the threshold (Judg. 19.27); the blood splashed on the wall, and the horses that trample it (2 Kgs 9.33). In the same way, the lyric poet may enter another person's situation. For example, an author puts the words of a poem in a dying man's mouth (Ps. 88). The authors of the psalms enter diverse situations in imagination, and thus create their poems (I refer here to original poems, not conventional ones made up of topics and reminiscences).

Now I go on to the reader. Among the majority of the exegetes, a deep-rooted distrust prevails with respect to the interpreter's imagination. They think that 'the crazy woman in the house' (Teresa of Avila) serves only to wander far from the text and from its authentic sense.

'These are fantasies, imagination!'—no better way to discredit a type of exegesis. It is, of course, a fact that imagination sometimes goes mad or wanders from the point. Many Midrashic commentaries entertain irrelevant excursions of fantasy: the dialogue in the country between Cain and Abel on the life to come, the demon Asael riding the serpent of Eden, and so on.[6]

However, no one should be condemned for a few lapses, since imagination is a necessary and excellent organ of comprehension and interpretation. Gunkel asked the exegete for a 'bridled fantasy' or a restrained imagination (*gezügelte Phantasie*),[7] and he was right, since what has been written with imagination must be read with imagination.

Later on, we shall see that language stylizes reality, articulating it and leaving intermediate spaces empty. Reducing the continuum of reality and experience, it generalizes at a basic level. It is up to imagination to fill in the empty spaces and return individual concretion to what is generic. Between the 'here–there–over there' of language, there are intermediate spaces perceived by the imagination, which can move to them in order to observe or revive.

This is far more so in the matter of the story. If the good narrator recreates a scene with two strokes of the brush, it is the reader's imagination that has to complete the facts. In two strokes, Isaiah the prophet summarizes war; 'boots that tread resoundingly, deranged blood-stained robes' (Isa. 9.4). Another poet goes and hears the pilgrims when they reach Jerusalem: 'our feet are now treading on your thresholds, Jerusalem' (Ps. 122.2). In order to hide spies, a village woman puts them in a dry well in the corral, 'took a blanket, spread it over the mouth of the well and scattered grain on it so that nothing was out of place' (2 Sam. 17.19). Relating the murder of Isbaal, the narrator offers us these two strokes: 'Isbaal was having an afternoon nap. The caretaker had fallen asleep while she was cleaning the wheat' (2 Sam. 4.5-6). It is up to the reader's imagination to complete or fill in the scenes. Historical accuracy is not expected for this, although neither is it forbidden. It is not necessary to recognize the original material of the

---

6. Many more can be read in the entertaining book by R. Graves and R. Patai, *Hebrew Myths: The Book of Genesis* (Garden City, NY: Doubleday, 1964). See also M. Pérez, *Los capítulos de Rabí Eliezer* (Valencia: Institución S. Jerónimo, 1984).

7. Gunkel, *Reden und Aufsätze*.

blanket, nor the agronomical species of the wheat, nor the exact conformation of the corral, but it is necessary to have some experience of the objects mentioned.

In the case of lyric, imagination acts by sympathy or empathy. Although not at death's door, imprisoned or exiled, the reader tries to live the corresponding emotions imaginatively, but without yielding to them. It is what Rahner calls 'vicarious experience'. Let us remember what happens to many watching a scene of violence or cruelty (if they are not hardened) at the cinema or on television. They feel as distressed as if it were real, their mouths go dry, they close their eyes. In these cases, they are watching a story, but this type of participation is more frequent in lyric poetry.

St Paul said to the Galatians: 'Put yourselves in my place, brethren, as I put myself in yours' (Gal. 4.12). The expression sounds familiar to us because we have heard it, and because we sometimes say it. It is an act of imagination to put oneself in the place of another, and is fundamental in the mutual knowledge of human beings. I do not put myself in the place of a rock or a chimpanzee. I share a conscious common nature with humans.

But is not imagination at variance with scholarship? Who would dare to affirm this today? Hypotheses are imaginative projections starting from a few facts, submitted later to the control of verification in virtue of the pending facts. Models are projections of the imagination to explain a defined complex of facts organically and 'metaphorically' and they remain submitted to revision (Kuhn called it a 'paradigm shift').

Until some decades ago, natural science was divided into theoretical and practical or experimental science. Theoretical science projects a hypothesis and proposes explanations that will one day be submitted to experimentation. Today an intermediate device is used: simulation on the computer. The prepared facts are put in the computer which receives the pertinent orders to 'experiment'. The instrument proceeds 'as if', and then offers answers with a high or variable rate of probability. The computer is a kind of 'mechanical imagination' (guided by a human being). Something similar may happen in our science when we use human non-mechanical imagination and accept the 'as if' in the explanation. Without affirming 'it is/it was thus', we decide that the text behaves 'as if', and that helps us to comprehend and explain. Honesty demands that we do not raise what we have understood 'as if', to the certainty of 'it is thus'.

There remain extreme cases in which the imagination creates objects, new beings such as the Sphinx, the centaur, the fire-spitting dragon. The Behemoth and the Leviathan of Job 41–42 are fantastical, but with traits taken from reality; so too are many figures of the Apocalypse fantastical. Imagination must be brought into play in order to grasp that imaginative world; but imagination must not be confined to the genre of fantasy.

Summary. What has been written with imagination must be read with imagination. The imagination is an extraordinary necessary organ of comprehension and interpretation, but must not be confounded with the genre of fantasy.

4. *Appropriation*

In the interpretation and comprehension of the literary work by the reader, there exists a further possibility to achieve an intimate communion of sense. Comprehension is not the highest achievement; the state denominated 'appropriation' should be reached.

Let us take a biblical example: Lk. 4.14-30. Jesus is present in the synagogue of Nazareth and, during the liturgical celebration, he reads some verses of ch. 61 of the book of Isaiah, a poem where an 'I' speaks. When he finishes reading he says, 'Today, in your presence, this scripture is fulfilled'. Jesus has appropriated the 'I' of the poem.

An extreme, and almost inevitable, case of appropriation is that of biblical psalms. In ancient times there was already an effort to identify the authors, the original people who had composed the poems: thence the titles that precede them. Let us approach the Christian context. In St Augustine, we find the frequent use of the formula *in persona N.* applied to the reading of the psalms. This ancient formula is perfectly understood when we approach the book of Psalms, because in the psalms, we normally meet an 'I' or a 'we' speaking . The psalms are originally written as prayers, and nearly always as available prayers, as an accessible repertory. They are written 'for all who find themselves in that situation'. The appropriation is already at the base of the psalm; this destiny to be appropriated is a native quality of the psalms.

In his classic commentary on the psalms, St Augustine repeats as a general principle that the psalms are pronounced by Christ. But how can Christ say 'Forgive my sin'? St Augustine finds a way out: in this case Christ speaks *in persona Ecclesiae*, because, being the head of the body, he can speak in its name.

The evangelist (Mk 15.34) puts Psalm 22 in the mouth of the crucified Christ: 'My God, my God, why have you forsaken me?' In this case, it means that the psalm must be read *in persona Christi morientis*. An appropriation is given, making possible another appropriation on the part of a member of the suffering Christ.

The concept *in persona N* is taken from the theatre, for the Greek term *prosopon* and the Latin *persona* denominate the ancient theatrical mask. The actor wore the mask to perform a part. There were different kinds of masks: the old man, the woman, the *miles gloriosus*. The actor wore one of them and played the 'part of', trying to give life to that particular character with his voice and gestures. In theatrical practice, two planes may be distinguished. In the exterior one I see a person, whom I may know, playing the part of Hippolitus: more profoundly I find that, in the poetical fable, Hippolitus represents a human type, and in a way acts *in persona* of a human type. Thanks to the actor's emotivity, to their voice, to their passion, the character has been alive for a few hours.

The actor appropriates their character on the stage. Many actors speak of absorption, of the search for the exact feelings and warm acting of the part. This demands a serious study of the character's traits and a sustained emotional effort. Today, before acting a part, actors often seek real experiences similar to the role they are going to represent in fiction, so as to have a better grasp of the reality of the character to which they are to give life on the stage. Those are cases of appropriation of great intensity but, even so, some may be disappointing. At the end of the play, the character dies, and immediately the actor reappears for a curtain call. The actor's appropriation was only a temporary fiction.

The case of someone who takes another's text to express their own sentiments may also help us to understand the theme of appropriation: the lover who finds a poem that he copies to send it to his loved one. The sentiments are there, the situation is common to the present lover and the previous one. The present one appropriates the language. Alternatively, take the case of the 'evangelists' of Guadalajara in Mexico, who reflect a custom very widespread in the past in times of illiteracy, or when culture was not widespread: there were people who wrote for others. Their action consisted not only in writing; in a way, the one who wrote the text became the person who asked to have it done.

Another case is that of popular poetry, in which the song is not a product of an amorphous community. Instead, the poets identify themselves with their people to such a point that the people consider them as the authors of those feelings and that language. Perhaps no one has expressed it better than Manuel Machado (1874–1947), writer of strictly popular *soleás* (a type of song):

> Until people sing them,
> folksongs are not folksongs;
> and when people sing them
> no one remembers the author.

> Such is the glory, Guillén,
> of those who write songs:
> hearing people say
> that no one has written them.

> Take care that your folksongs
> reach the hands of the people,
> even if they cease to be yours
> to belong to everyone else.

> So that on merging the heart
> with the popular soul,
> the name that is lost
> is won for eternity.[8]

It is not only that a reader has an experience and, seeking words with which to express it, finds a text that pleases them and takes it over (like the previous example of the lover who comes across the poem that says what he feels, but that he does not know how to say). Besides this, the text can mediate the reader's analogous experience, so long as there is a basic disposition.

Readers allow themselves to be interpellated by the text, and liberate their personal reply, evincing the impact caused by the written word. The appropriation of a text is not only reading through it, in various possible ways (out loud, alone in silence, with others). The appropriation of a text means opening oneself to it, receiving it as a source of personal meditation.

---

8.   Manuel Machado, 'Canto a Andalucía', *Poemas* (Madrid: Alianza, 1979).

On the level of the believer, given the distance and novelty that Christian faith supposes with respect to the Old Testament, it seems that some texts are irrelevant. Curiously, the Church accepts the book of Psalms completely, adding hardly any lyrical passages of liturgy to the New Testament. This is because the Church already possessed its repertoire of prayers, namely the Psalter, which, on being appropriated by the New Testament, had become new. However, an adjustment of horizons is necessary, horizons of experience with a view to expression. For this task, symbols (which I shall speak about later) offer themselves as useful mediators.

I have said that we want an appropriation that goes even further than that of the absorbed actor. We seek an authentic appropriation. For example, liturgical action is not a stage performance. It must not be ephemeral in the sense of the theatre, but authentic appropriation. If we do not attain it we shall be present at a farce, no matter how well it is acted and no matter how professionally it is done. This is the touchstone of the psalms. If we believe they are the Word of God, as the prayers of the Christian community, we may reach them only through appropriation.

We may distinguish two basic forms of appropriation. The first is the more extreme: I rigorously make the text mine. I take Psalm 51, I make that situation, those sentiments and the language it expresses mine.

The second appears when we do not find ourselves in that specific situation reflected in the text. At that moment I am not at death's door but by means of sym/pathy, com/passion, solidarity, I want to participate with a dying brother and recite Psalm 88.

The psalms searchingly pose the problem of Christian sense in the Old Testament and the problem of appropriation. These are problems that are imposed on us as hermeneutical exigency, and reveal to us both their theological and spiritual relevance.

Summary. We may seek an appropriation of the text in literary comprehension and interpretation. The text already understood can also mediate the reader's analogous experience and its expression. In the Christian sphere, the psalms stand out as a particular example of the need for appropriation.

Chapter 7

LANGUAGE

1. *Introduction*

In tracing a curve that goes from the author to the reader by means of
language, I have arrived at a significant point in my picture of
hermeneutics. Although people communicate with their fellow beings
by different means, the most important is language. Communication is
also possible by physical contact or proximity, by gestures such as
embraces, kisses and shaking hands, and, at exceptional moments, that
communication has greater value; for example, a hand resting silently
on the shoulder of someone who has suffered a loss. Communication
comes with looks, which may be of radiant intensity, and the simple
tone of the voice; but there is nothing like language.

Human beings are animals of articulated speech. By speaking they
are fulfilled and manifest themselves as bodily spirit, because language
is corporeal and spiritual.

However, there has been no lack of people, including writers, who
have denied or minimized the capacity of language for communication.
In his 'Letter to a Young Poet', Rilke says that 'all that happens to us is
inexpressible. Basically and precisely for what is essential, we are
unspeakably alone'. Roubakine, the philosopher, said at the beginning
of the century that 'of books nobody knows more than the impressions
and opinions he has of them'. The critic Maurice Blanchot fights
against the paradox that 'all direct communication by means of language is impossible'. And Paul Valéry affirms: 'Tout ce qui peut se dire
est nul' (Everything that can be said is valueless).[1] And yet movement
is proved by walking, and communication by language is proved by
talking (we shall come back to this theme).

---

1. See Ray, *Literary Meaning*.

As a shared social asset, language is the condition of possibility of articulated communication and, at the same time, conditions this communication. Language surpasses us before and behind, outside—and also inside? It existed before us; in it we were born and grew, learnt to think, and in it we move with everyone else. It survives us and is broader than our mental world. Is it also more profound or radical? If we need language in order to think, then the answer should be affirmative.

But since we neither invented it nor have exclusive possession of it, language conditions us in general and in every individual act. If there is anything absolute in the truth of a judgment, that truth is conditioned when it enters a specific language. It does not turn false—God forbid!—it is simply conditioned by the language in which it is expressed; and without language it cannot be expressed.

Even mathematical language must be submitted in a way to this law. A mathematical formula is conditioned by the base on which it is expressed. For example, 12 means twelve units in the decimal system: in a system based on 6, 20 would express the same value, and in a system based on 2, it would be written 1100. What happens is that, dealing with fairly small numbers, the referent is precise and unchangeable, whereas, in a language that is not mathematical, the referent is seen in a special way, showing a particular facet which is variable according to the systems.

2. What Is Language?

How is language related to reality and to our experience? Here, I do not propose a systematic treatise, neither philosophical nor linguistic, of language. Instead, I pay attention only to aspects of language that have specifically to do with this hermeneutical reflection.

First of all, let us clear the way of false ideas: naive and pseudo-scientific conception. Naive thinking—or not thinking—considers language as a simple reproduction of reality, even though its conventional forms vary. The Germans say 'Baum', the English 'tree', the Greek 'dendron', the Spaniards 'árbol'; but all of them say the same thing because we name an object that 'is' what we 'say'. We use the conditional, causal or temporary clause because the two happenings are thus related: one is principal and the other dependent. In modern terminology we would formulate it like this: according to the languages we change the signifier, but the signified is identical. The mental worlds of different languages are exactly transposed, because they naturally correspond with reality.

When God shows all the animals to Adam (Gen. 2), that first father gives them their exact names, 'whatever the man called each living creature, that should be its name'; and so the zoological classification is fixed, once and for all. Did he do the same with the plants? No, because he needed another kind of company, human company (here I do not analyse the subject of a protolanguage as the imposition of names or a catalogue of labels).

Few educated people will hold with such a naive conception of language, but they may feel attracted by an opposite conception, which seems scientific. It consists in applying the theory of the media to language. Supposing there is an oral or visual message, we translate it, codify it in electromagnetic impulses that we send in series of waves. An instrument receives these sequences of modulated waves and retranslates them into images and sounds which the spectator watches and listens to. The medium does not affect the message in any way at all, if the transmitting and receiving instruments work properly.

In pseudo-scientific thinking, language is conceived of in this way. A pre-verbal message is translated and codified into language; the receiver decodifies it, rejects the medium/language, and retains the message intact. Language has no effect whatsoever on the message. The technical analogy and terminology ('codify', 'decodify', 'electro-magenetic impulses', etc.) confer an air of respectability on the explanation. However, because it seems scientific, such an explanation is no less false. In fact, it is more dangerous.

The truth is that language substantially affects the message. There is no completely constituted pre-verbal message that language transports as a neutral vehicle. Language is rather like a mould that models the message.

Another error to be corrected is the atomistic conception of language which isolates each word and places it in a linear relationship with the expressed object; or in a triangular relationship with the concept, and, through it, with the object (we must remember that the signified of a word is not the object, but rather the concept). The isolated word is an artificial product. The word lives in the society of a language united by multiple relationships. It belongs to a lexical field and to a semantic field, it belongs to a tradition, and may be charged with historical or literary connotations. A word is a point of intersection between multiple interwoven lines, both in the sphere of language (*langue*) and in that of discourse (*parole*).

3. *Language as Stylization*

Let us take a folding metre ruler, divided into ten connected articulated decimeter segments. With it we try to outline a circumference. Impossible! A circumference is theoretically a continuous line of unidimensional points equidistant from a centre. Between the decangle and the circumference are empty separating spaces. Let us reduce the segments of the folding ruler to five centimetres. We get nearer, but cannot form the circumference. Let us make segments of one centimetre: we still cannot form the circumference. The articulated ruler does not coincide with the continuous line. This analogy helps us to describe language as an articulated set with a relative economy of segments.

Now let us consider the lexical plane. Although the lexical field is the most numerous system of a language and is always open (so long as the language does not die), each semantic field and even more the lexical field, operates by the law of economy. Space is continuous in itself and in my experience. Language offers me 'near, far, here, there, beyond, inside, outside, centre, periphery, extreme' and not much more. I have to manage with this in order to communicate with others. The space around me is circular and continuous. I have 'front, behind, right, left'. What can I communicate with these? This is the basis of the law of economy—language stylizes reality and experience.

Let us consider a language with morphological inflection like Spanish. The time that crosses us lengthways is continuous. Our verbal system offers us the imperfect, past historic, perfect, past perfect, present, future and perfect future. Why is there not a form for the durative or reiterative future like the imperfect for the past? A 'was' in the future. The inflection system is perfectly constructed and closed.

In syntax, apart from the simple sentence and the predicative sentence with the copulative 'to be', we have the temporal, causal, consecutive, final or conditional sentence; and also the enunciative, exclamatory or optative sentence. Are all the relationships of reality and my experience reduced to these? Let us notice, incidentally, the frequent indecision between final and consecutive, between conditional and temporal. The syntactical structure is also closed.

Stylization does not mean deformation. It means simplification and economy. It means making the language possible as an identifiably manageable system, apt for communication. However, by stylizing, we achieve only an approximation.

To this is added the fact that articulation varies from language to language, on the planes of the lexicon, morphology and syntax. There is nothing better than translating to appreciate these differences, which belong to internal articulation, not only to external expression. Above all, it is structures of meaning that do not coincide from language to language (neither a previous nor a basic language exists). However, is it impossible to go back to a zone where perfect coincidence can be found?

4. *Overcoming the Limits?*

Admitting that language always conditions enunciations and that these therefore change their meaning when the language changes, we uneasily ask: 'But is there not a permanent immutable nucleus?' Let us imagine partly overlapping circles where there is an identical zone common to both, which may be separated. Is that not how we translate? We take the coinciding zone since we cannot make the circles completely coincide. Translation would not be possible otherwise. In languages we distinguish deep structures from the surface ones. At that deep level, is there not a coincidence that emerges afterwards in a different superficial form? This is so *a fortiori* when it is to do with technical language endowed with precise stable terms that may be translated very exactly, even if they enter a new normal linguistic system.

I am going to suggest two paths to attain the unity or coincidence of two languages: remotion and reduction. If they do not work, I shall propose a third.

Imagine a basic enunciation that is clear and defined in its system. When it passes to another language or another epoch, elements such as connotations or contextual associations adhere to it. It would be sufficient to remove the adherences in order to recover the original unchanged nucleus. This supposes that the initial nucleus had not yet changed when it passed to the new system. However, this is supposing too much, because the new system affects the unity it receives.

We come up with two enunciations or autonomous elaborations of a fact, an experience or a mystery. We try to reduce them to a common denominator, a third enunciation to pair off disparate elements and resolve the differences. The task is a difficult one. We would have to remove partial components of both, so as to transfer the residue to a new enunciation. On removing contextual elements we modify the residue. Something is sacrificed, something is saved.

The third path is perhaps more frequent, but is not usually mentioned. What is permanent is broad and global; what changes is its narrowing. A generic inclusive enunciation, or one that is only scarcely differentiated or symbolic, is shared without difficulty and with no appreciable change. Differences emerge when this enunciation begins to narrow and become precise, and sometimes the two expressions become irreconcilable.

'The Holy Spirit spoke through the prophets' is an enunciation of the Creed, shared by many confessions and schools. How is it to be understood? As soon as the question is put and research begins, diverging answers emerge, as well as explanations that are sometimes conflicting.

Project the three solutions in the image of overlapping circles. According to the first solution, the new circle is put on top of an inscribed concentric circle, which is the unchangeable nucleus, recoverable by the removal of the circles placed on top. In the second solution, we have two juxtaposed circles. We superimpose them and take away what does not coincide. In the third solution, we have a large circle within which there are various small ones that are separate or partly coincide. We leave these out of consideration and keep the large permanent circle.

We illustrate this with the text in Mt. 26.26: 'This is my body', an enunciation that is not differentiated: a mortal body or a glorified one? Does 'is' tell us the identity of the subject and the predicate or is it a metaphorical equivalence? The scholastics sought exact definitions and concordant interpretations. Let us see how Duns Scotus explains it:

> There are three possible ways of conceiving the Body of Christ in the sacred form: 1. The substance of the Body of Christ is in the host simultaneously with the substance of the bread. 2. The substance of the bread has been destroyed to give place to the substance of the Body of Christ. 3. The substance of the bread has been transformed into the substance of the Body of Christ.[2]

2.   Duns Scotus, *In librum Sententiarum*, IV, 11.3 n. 5.

According to Scotus's analysis, the three opinions 'explain suffi-
ciently the text of Scripture'. Furthermore, from a philosophical and
rational point of view, the first two explain the mystery in an easier and
more adequate way, but the third opinion must be preferred, '...*sicut
tenet sancta romana ecclesia*'.

Thus in the Lateran Council (1215); Trent makes the *totius substantia
panis* even more precise, incorporating the Aristotelian theory of
substance and accidents (1551). The question is philosophical and has
dogmatic value. In the search for greater and greater precision, confessions are separated, as well as the schools within them, and further, the
authors within these. What is permanent is not a nucleus but the contrary, the broad, undifferentiated circle.

Is it better not to ask questions then? It is not better, it is not human.
Faith wants to understand and does so by asking and answering. Is
there a criterion of truth and accuracy? How far is the difference that of
a school and when does it start to be that of a confession? It is not my
concern to speak of criteria, but rather to describe a process in the
context of our reflection on language and its interpretation.

5. *Language between Author and Reader (Producer and Receiver)*

In order for communication to work, the two participants in the process
must have a common language. This is a condition of possibility.
However, since the knowledge of language by both is not identical, the
mediating language actually conditions comprehension. If the author is
a person of letters, their grasp of language is probably greater than the
reader's: but not completely, for active and passive knowledge must
be distinguished. Average readers usually know far more words and
expressions than those they normally use, and are capable of recognizing them when they are used by an author.

Progress must also be taken into account, that is to say, knowledge of
a language is not static, but grows with contact and practice. The more
one reads an author, reads their language, the more one gets to know
and control it. Language conditions comprehension, and repeated comprehension makes language more efficient as a means of communication.

Another factor that is difficult to define precisely is what we may call
'sensitivity to language'. This is not simply knowledge of the language
in question, but the pleasurable appreciation of its phonetic, rhythmic,

expressive and descriptive values. There are people who enjoy and appreciate the language of Shakespeare or Cervantes for its own sake, and do not pay attention exclusively to the story or the characters. This is a privileged condition for the understanding of good writers.

When the author and the reader do not share a language, two ways are open: the reader learns the author's language or an interpreter translates it. It is clear that translation is not the substitution of each word in the original text for a word in the receiving language, which is what Aquila and the Bible of Ferrara did. The exercise and result of translating expose many essential aspects of hermeneutical theory.

Summary. Language is a means of articulated communication among human beings. It is a condition of possibility, as well as a conditioning factor: possibility against those who declare it impotent on the part of the author or the reader (producer–receiver); conditioning against the naive conception of language as simple reproduction of reality, and against the pseudo-scientific conception which considers language as the neutral code of a previously constituted sense, and against the atomistic conception which reduces language to atoms or monads. Language stylizes reality and experience (the image of the folding ruler)—it is the law of articulation and economy. Attempts are made to make it more flexible, articulate it more, so that it comes nearer: by division and subdivision, by the combination of elements (syntagmas).

Language conditions enunciations, which change meaning when the language is changed.

6. *Language and Theme*

In the artificial diagram, Language and Theme occupy extreme positions on a vertical line. How, in fact, are they related?

In the Bible, the theme is God who reveals God's self as a mystery, or the mystery of human salvation, or the mysterious human experience of divine action. Does a language capable of approaching such a sublime theme exist? There are those who reply in the negative, and the study of their objections will serve us as a guideline to give an affirmative answer.

In positivism. The criterion of the validity of language is the theme, if it is verifiable, otherwise language speaks senselessly. Verifiable means empirically controllable. However, the supposed 'metaphysical' realities are not 'physically' empirically verifiable, and therefore meta-physical language is meaningless. It is a game that is closed and exhausted within itself, like the game of tennis without a ball in Antonioni's film *Blow Up* (1967).

Religious language is metaphysical. God and God's revelation and action are not empirically verifiable: our experience is verifiable, but it has no transcendental object. Religious language has no sense because it has no real theme.

The answer to this extreme positivism is given to us by the defence of metaphysics, perhaps through a transcendental reduction, in other words, ascending to the conditions of possibility. In the question, transcendence is already implicitly present.[3]

Without being a strict demonstration, the confessional answer has its value. We cultivate hermeneutical reflection in the interior of our faith and based on it, not before it. In other words, we include it in the framework of exegetical activity, not in fundamental theology.

In *transcendentalism*. The self-revealed God and our experience of God are so mysterious and so far beyond us that they are unutterable. Whatever language is tried, even the biblical language itself, is totally inadequate: it veils more than it unveils, it deforms more than it forms. Humankind may respond to God's interpellation only with a total global attitude that we shall call faith. The moment humans attempt to objectify any content in it, they deform it irremediably. Does not Job agree?

> If only you would hold your tongues
> that indeed would be wisdom! (Job 13.5)

> Are you not daunted by his majesty
> and crushed by his terror? (Job 13.11)

The same Job confesses in the end: 'I knew of you by report; now my eyes have beheld you', but he does not tell us what he has seen.

Apart from the symbol, biblical language concerned with God works with polarities, opposing affirmations that allow us to place God and compel us to conceive God beyond distinction and opposition (transcends all categories). God is father and mother, repents and does not repent, is far and near, without and within. In everything said about God and about experience of God, it is always essential to remember

3.   Cf. E. Coreth, *Die Frage nach der Frage*; J. Ladrière, *L'articulation du sens: Discours scientifique et parole de la foi* (Paris: Cerf, 1970).

that a mystery is being considered: 'We propose the wisdom of God as mystery' (1 Cor. 2.7). When God reveals himself, it is not that God is no longer a mystery, but that God is revealed as a mystery.

I have spoken of God and our experience, because our deepest richest experiences surpass our consciousness and exceed our capacity for expressing them. Not only the common person but also the poet, who masters the instrument, complains of the inadequacy of language to 'express what I feel'. In a text of Werner Bergengruen (1892–1964), the German poet and prose writer, we read:

> Making poetry is like conversing in a foreign language we barely master. We do not say what we would wish to and what we should, but only the little we are capable of expressing. Even the most apt and best chosen word is a mere cipher, a shorthand sign. It is distressing for man to perceive the poorness and inadequacy of language. Yet he should be grateful that what he is conceded of cordial sentiments and sensorial and spiritual experiences is always greater than his capacity for expressing it.[4]

The answer to this strong objection of transcendentalism lies in the great principle of analogy, the metaphysical analogy of being and the poetic analogy of the symbol. The Bible normally proceeds along the second way, which is chronologically prior. In the confessional setting, the Bible responds to the objection with its mere presence.

It is strange that biblical authors do not speak of the difficulty in expressing their mysterious experiences. Jeremiah once protests that 'he does not know how to speak'; but the reason is his fear of the prophet's dangerous vocation, because his oracles show his great creative capacity and mastery of poetical resources. Moses complains of being clumsy in speech, and the reason was similar; he wanted to elude the mission of confronting the Pharaoh. Only Paul speaks of a man (himself) who 'heard words so secret that human lips may not repeat them' (2 Cor. 12.4).

Other objections against the validity of language are the closed character of the sign, studied by semiotics; the lack of affirmation or negation in literary language, the instrument of poetic language. I prefer to deal with these questions when I treat the text and its relationship with language.

4.   W. Bergengruen, *Das Geheimnis Verbleist* (Zürich: Arche, 1952).

7. *Scientific and Literary Language*

Refining language. It seems that, in my desire to show how it conditions language, I have seen fit to point out the poverty, distance, inadequacy and approximate character of language. But, is that all? Is it not possible to improve the situation?

a. *Language as an Instrument*

Let us return to the previous comparison. We divided the decimetres by half and then into centimetres. We do something similar with the lexicon of language. We divide and subdivide concepts and names, we differentiate a lexical field, we add words at the extremes of the series or in its interstices. If our eyes distinguish more than a thousand colours, and the list of colours in our language contains seven (red, orange, yellow, green, blue, indigo, violet), we insert others separating red into vermilion, carmine, crimson, reddish, cinnabar. Not content with this, we add words to obtain nuances. The adjective modifies the noun, the adverb modifies the verb and the adjective.

Scientific language constantly invents terms to distinguish and define; but above all, it is poets and writers who refine language and make it more and more capable of expressing what was previously inexpressible:

> a heavy clumsy giant
> the happy weariness of living it (life)
> standing and slowly dying
> and a sudden tremulous hand makes the foliage palpitate

Let us consider the contributions of the symbolist and surrealist schools. Thanks to them, the instrument of poetic language has become more flexible, more versatile and more refined.

b. *The Nature and Conditions of Both Languages*

We may speak of two ways of approaching language. It is worthwhile proposing extreme cases (scholars and writers) for the distinction, even though we usually only find approximations and predominances.

Scholars distance themselves from language. If it does not work for them, they streamline and refine it: it is merely an instrument that they handle and keep subject to them. It is a transmitter of sense, not a producer, although a conceptual and terminological repertory has also been of use to scholars for thinking.

Writers have a vital relationship with language. They feel immersed in it without drowning; they feel it in their pens (machines, computers) as a producer of sense; and in turn feel themselves creative with regard to it, both factors to a different degree.

Scholars trim their language for pure information. They strive (or should strive) for precision and clarity, when the theme and the state of the research permit it. Their relationship with language is rational, not emotive. The use they make of their language is often in order to manipulate reality; other times, it is moved by the pure desire to know.

Writers cultivate a subjective relationship with their language, and at the same time, an inclusive one that tries to exploit the potentialities of their language. Writers seek their own participation, as well as the readers'.

c. *Both Languages Draw away, Each One in its Own Way*

Scholars practise a distance that is neutral, either spontaneously or by inhibition, like the surgeon who operates on their son as just another patient. Writers use calculated distance as a particular form of relationship; for example, in irony, humour or pathetic coldness. Scientific language is usually literal and abstract, rich in terms, nouns and copulative clauses. Literary language is usually concrete, often metaphoric and even may give concrete value to abstract nouns.

The images of scientific language are secondary, didactic and subsequent to an already constituted sense. The images of literary language are constitutive; a means of access to reality and experience.

Centuries ago, mediaeval scholastics distinguished the *modi* of science and literature. Scholastic science worked with the *definitivus*, *divisivus* and *collectivus modi*. Literature (the Bible) worked with the *narrativus*, *praeceptivus/prohibitivus*, *comminatorins/deprecatorius*, and *laudativus modi* in another version: *praeceptivus*, *exemplificativus*, *exhortativus*, *revelativus* and *orativus*.[5] As can be seen, the first catalogue is brief and exact; in the second, the mediaeval scholastics moved with uncertainty; but it is interesting that they appreciated the basic difference. Moreover, in their commentaries, they devote enormous effort to transforming biblical *modi* into scholastic ones, especially in defining and dividing.

---

5. Cf. Alonso Schökel, *The Inspired Word*, pp. 103-105.

8. *Language: From One to Another*

a. *From One Language to Another*

A language establishes and maintains communication between two interlocutors when the language is common to both, insofar as it is common. And when the language is not common and not shared? We have already said it: either one approaches an unknown language by studying it, or someone translates the text or acts as interpreter in the conversation. In each solution, a common language is established or re-established. If such a common sharing is established, the language mediates the communication without the need for any other mediation. Very often, but especially in conversation, we do not even notice the medium: as with the air that surrounds us, as with the sounds we hear without paying attention to the mediation of the air that transmits the vibrations. When for any reason immediate communication fails, then we realize the function of the medium: we have to repeat, articulate better, clarify, contribute a synonym, find the meaning of an idiom, etc.

The biblical texts were written in Hebrew and Greek (and a very few in Aramaic). Today, most readers read the Bible in a translation, that is to say, an interpreter has intervened and given an acceptable substitute.

Once we have the Bible in English, readers discover there are many things they do not understand. Because of the theme being handled, the presuppositions or the literary peculiarities, it turns out that the English text is not a mediator of meaning and communication. Let us look at an example:

> Place cairns, set up signposts,
> make sure of the road which you will tread,
> return, maid of Israel, return to your cities.
> How long are you going to hesitate, elusive maiden?
> For the Lord creates again in the land,
> and woman will embrace man (Jer. 31.21-22).

Although it is in proper English and all the sentences are understandable, is this important text understood? Now that we do not understand the English text, we understand that we do not understand. Before now, we could put it down to the unfamiliar Hebrew. This is where the role of the exegete comes in, proposing an *explicative interpretation.* But take heed, that interpreter's only mission is to establish immediate communication between text and reader, and make comprehension of the text possible. The explanation should not supplant the text.

At this point, we need to speak of the passing from one language to another in the framework of explanation (not of translation in the strict sense of the word).

b. *From One Literary Language to Another*

One device of explanation is paraphrasing, which provides the text with synonyms, clarifying what is obscure, expressing what is implied, amplifying what is concise, revealing allusions. One type of paraphrasing is the targum, which translated from Hebrew to Aramaic, with free amplifications and with the addition of small wedges of free creation.

Is paraphrasing legitimate? It has been called heresy, which, in a sense, is true. If the interpreter wants to supplant the text with paraphrase, they commit heresy, but if, by means of paraphrasing, they make comprehension easier and lead the reader back to the text, they render a great service. Very often there is no better commentary than the respectful paraphrase.

> Purpúreas rosas sobre Galatea
> la Alba entre lirios cándidos deshoja.[6]

> Purple roses over Galatea
> Dawn among white lilies plucks.

José Ruiz Medrano paraphrases: 'La Alba, en su personificación maravillosa, derrama rosas rojas y lirios blancos para amasar el cuerpo de Galatea' (Dawn, in her marvellous personification, strews red roses and white lilies to knead Galatea's body).

> Tal, antes que la opaca nube rompa,
> previene rayo fulminante trompa.[7]

> Before the opaque cloud breaks,
> a trumpet forewarns of the fulminating thunderbolt.

'Antes de que se rompa el seno de la negra nube, preñada de tempestad, una trompa (trompeta) es el heraldo que precede y anuncia la descarga del rayo fulminante' (José Ruiz Medrano). ('Before the womb of the black cloud, pregnant with tempest, breaks, a trumpet is the herald that precedes and announces the discharge of the fulminating thunderbolt'.)

---

6.   L. de Góngora (1561–1627), 'Polifemo'.
7.   De Góngora, 'Polifemo'.

Analysis, which may embrace grammar, lexicon, syntax, rhetoric and poetry, is different from paraphrase. A great part of our modern exegesis consists in analysis. One part becomes scientific, or even technical language; another part is a conveyance of pertinent cultural information. It is supposed and hoped that, with the text explained in this way, the reader may contend with it directly.

Sometimes the paraphrase or commentary is prolonged on its own account to such a point that the partly explained text is converted into the stimulus of a new creation. In his second epistle to the Corinthians Paul takes the text of Moses' radiance to start a reflection on the apostle's vocation (2 Cor. 3–4 and Exod. 33–34); the epistle to the Hebrews takes a couple of texts on Melchizedek to argue concerning the priesthood of Christ (Heb. 7; Gen. 14.17-20 and Ps. 110). Something of the original text is explained because the significant power of its symbols is revealed, but the result is a new autonomous text. The usual and very fitting term for this is 'midrash'.

A rigorous way of passing from literary to scientific language is transforming symbols into concepts, sensorial images into spiritual concepts or abstract terms.[8] I proceed systematically and with examples.

In Psalm 51, the sinner tries to express his repentance, that is, that sentiment lodged within him that seems to disintegrate his spirit and break up what was compact. His will was as firm and tenacious as a rock; now it falls apart and disintegrates into dust. The person at prayer says 'his heart is crushed or ground' by the intensity of the sorrow for what he has done. In Spanish there is a similar expression: 'estoy hecho polvo' (I am pulverized). A physical image of the stone that is smashed and ground up, serves as a symbol to express an experience impossible or difficult to express any other way. Greek and Latin translations used a verb that preserved its imaginative expression. The scholastics laid hold of the symbol and transformed it into the *concept contritio* (with the same root), with no imaginative residue. Since the *definitio* does not suffice them, they resort to a *divisio* and, according to the formal motive of repentance, distinguish between *contritio* and *attritio*. Both concepts acquire precision and constancy of terms in a system.

Science needs a repertoire of terms in order to think and operate. Theological science is not foreign to this exigency. Exegetical science

---

8.   Concerning this, it is useful to see G. Söhngen's interesting work, *Analogie und Metapher* (Munich: Karl Alber, 1962), in which the passing of the symbol to the concept and from the concept to the term are clearly explained.

also has recourse to this exercise, although to a lesser degree. We extract concepts from the symbol, and we fix concepts in terms. That is how it must be. In the process, we gain precision and stability. But precision comes from *prae-cidere*, which means to cut away: many elements are excised in favour of a rigorously outlined piece.

The activity is legitimate and necessary. The danger consists, first, in wanting to substitute the literary text for conceptualized extracts; secondly, in working exclusively with those conceptual products, drawing further and further away from its literary matrix (I return to the theme when I speak about the symbol).

From scholastic theology, as an exemplary case, we pass on to another type of scientific transformation. In Psalm 39, we read: 'like the moth, you eat away his treasures/his attractiveness'. It is terrible to see human existence like precious cloth at the mercy of silently voracious insects, and more terrible to feel that that hidden moth is God, the author of 'human fabric' (Ps. 139). However, on coming to the corresponding Hebrew term another 'scientific' explanation is possible: the Hebrew word refers to a *lepidopteron* of the *tineida* family, the *Tiena pelionella* or the *Tricophaga tapetiella* (ancient translators confounded it with the spider). The second explanation identifies the insect with maximum precision; the first explanation expresses the significant poetic function of the image in paraphrase. Which of the two explanations is better? More objective? If 'objective' is what responds to its object and the object is a poem; the first should be preferred. This does not always happen in exegetical practice.

It is not the same to spiritualize as conceptualize, because 'spiritual' is not the same as 'abstract'. 'He was trembling' is a concrete physical description; 'he was afraid' is a concrete spiritual effect. Trembling is opposed to confidence and courage which are abstract spiritual concepts. Biblical narrative and lyric tend towards what is concrete in itself or as a symbol of spiritual intimacy. The Septuagint version (of the Seventy) and, in its wake, the Vulgate, carried out an enormous task of spiritualizing, and bequeathed their results to their successors. Many modern translators fail to break the secular crust in order to recover physical realism, the expressiveness of the original biblical language:

> *Anima eorum tabescebat in malis*
> his soul dissolved with evils (spiritualized)
> his stomach was upset (physical)

> *Intraverunt aquae usque ad animam meam*
> the waters entered as far as my soul (spiritualized)
> I was up to my neck in water (physical)

With great fervour many mediaeval commentators, especially monks, continued the exercise of spiritualizing biblical language. Contemporaneously, scholastics conceptualized it, and the *lectio monastica* and the *lectio scholastica*[9] followed parallel paths.

In conclusion, if we wish to comprehend the Bible, we must comprehend its language, both in translation and in the original. It is not worth peeling the language of the Bible to consume the fruit; it is not worth stripping it of its bark, because the sap circulates in the bark (pith, cambium); it must not be skinned, but rather caressed. Meaning does not lie behind language, but is in it. Language gives shape, configures meaning. Language is not a ghostly veil nor the docetic appearance of pure spirit.

Summary. We have examined language with regard to the theme, specifically the transcendent biblical theme. Positivism declares it meaningless, because its theme is metaphysical and empirically non-verifiable. Transcendentalism also declares it totally inadequate because its theme is mystery. The answer lies in metaphysical analogy or poetical symbol.

Transit from one language to another is translation. From one literary language to another, paraphrase, prolongation. From literary language to scientific language, symbol, concept, term; corporal/spiritual, concrete/abstract.

9. *On Illocution*

By illocution I understand the attitude of the speaker in making an utterance. The exposition therefore belongs to the sphere of language, in borderline areas of pragmatics and the purpose of the author. A recent book[10] proposes these concise definitions:

9.   Cf. L. Alonso Schökel and C. Carniti, *Salmos*, I (Estella: Verbo Divino, 1992), pp. 40-44.

10. J. Thomas, *Meaning in Interaction* (London: Longmans, Green & Co., 1995).

Locution:	the actual words uttered
Illocution:	the force or intention behind the words
Perlocution:	the effect of the illocution on the hearer

Let us begin with an example. In one text we find these phrases: 'I gave them unsound precepts, commandments that will not give them life. I have corrupted them with the offerings they made immolating their firstborn' (Ezek. 20.15-26).

The sentence is clear, but precisely because of its clarity, it is incredible that God should have pronounced it. The intepreter examines the sentence thoroughly. Is it affirmative or interrogative? In Spanish, a question is enclosed between two punctuation marks. It is delimited, and defined by writing '¿...?' In other languages, we often discern the interrogative value at the very end, when we come up against the solitary question mark ...? The writing tells us how the speaker pronounces the sentence, how they understand and interpret it. What happens in a language that does not have these punctuation marks? E. Vogt has suggested reading the verses cited by Ezekiel as a question. Is that the solution? No, because then we still have to face the question. We normally ask a question to obtain information we need from someone else. Is this how God asks? We cannot say that God speaks to obtain information God needs from people. The exegete explains that it is a rhetorical question which demands a negative answer. It is an emphatic way of affirming by interpellation. The Spaniard will make it explicit starting with 'acaso' (Is it that...?) Is it that I gave them unsound precepts? Of course not. We have resorted to a rhetorical figure to explain how the subject speaks. It is a common rhetorical figure which many peoples had used before the Greeks labelled and catalogued it. It is perfectly translatable. Of course, spoken language has melodic or tonal designs to distinguish different types of questions.

These examples show us the importance of knowing this aspect in order to ensure correct communication. From these we may go on to others that are broader and more complex.

Let us suppose that we have witnessed an unusual incident: an accident or a mishap prevented by someone's courage. We tell friends or companions about it. The following day, we read a report of the happening in the daily paper. After a few weeks, a judge summons us to give testimony about what happened, and we tell it once more. Although my version and that in the newspaper coincide in essentials, they differ in many things. My version for friends and that given to the judge may be almost identical. Even so, the way of making the utterance is different. For friends and for the judge it is oral with resources of intonation; that of the reporter is written, with a public function that is not judicial. To my friends I simply narrate, to the judge I give testimony. Thus we have three ways of making the utterance. To this example may be added that of a novelist who adapts the story and incorporates it into a novel.

The way of making the utterance, or illocution notably affects total communication. Although the contents of the information are equivalent, what the text means changes. Knowledge of illocution is important, perhaps essential, in order to comprehend and explain a text. The case of testimony in a process crosses into the field of pragmatics.

Let us return to the case of the question. I question someone because I want to know something, receive information or get guidance. In an examination, the teacher asks to find out what the pupils know and doe not know, and marks their papers thus. A judge interrogates in order to verify facts and responsibilities. In class the teacher asks so as to arouse the attention of the pupils (a didactic question). The orator feigns ignorance when asking so as to impress the listeners with their knowledge (a rhetorical question). Perhaps the grammatical and written forms of all these types of question are identical, but the oral intonation would probably be different. Illocution is definitely different, ordered so as to know or evaluate or ascertain or move.

> I shall deliver them from the power
> of the Abyss, I shall rescue them from Death (Hos. 13.14 LXX)

> Shall I deliver them from the power of the Abyss,
> Shall I rescue them from Death? (Hebrew)

Both these sentences are the same, except that the former affirms and the latter refuses by means of a rhetorical question. The change is produced by the form of the utterance, that is, by illocution. The second phrase is a translation from the original Hebrew; the first, from the Greek version. In 1 Cor. 15.55, Paul follows the Greek text.

We appreciate the importance of illocution as a factor of global communication, and we also observe how it invades the sphere of the aim pursued by the author. When only the text is available to us, it is necessary to examine the immediate or mediate context. This may be difficult when ancient texts or those of other cultures are being dealt with. We lack precisely expressed indications (illocution is implied, not stated). Very often we must face the risk of an activity considered to be subjective, or we have to proceed by trial and error.

Let us move on to wisdom literature, which we find filled with imperatives and evaluations. The grammar is univocal. Has the text been understood? If we look at the contents, we find proverbs that 'command' the same things as legal code, but is the communication identical?

Once again we resort to illocution theory. Several times the Old Testament defends the boundaries of family property: Deut. 19.14; 27.17; Hos. 5.10; Job 24.2; Prov. 15.25; 22.28; 23.10. Do they all say the same thing? Perhaps the material contents are the same, but not the illocutionary force. Deut. 19.14 legislates or quotes a law; Deut. 27.17 invokes a curse against the transgressor (who is perhaps clandestine); Hos. 5.10 is prophetic; Job makes a bitter polemical reflection; Proverbs advises. The legislator has political power and can interpret the word of entailment juridically to the subjects, while the sapiential doctor offers advice from experience.

All this must be held in mind in order to comprehend and explain. In many cases, the context defines illocution: the political, juridical, family or cultic situation. If it is important to identify the speaker in order to comprehend the psalms, it may also be important to listen to how the speaker utters the words.

The historian wants to relate deeds that have happened; the novelist wants to present probable or fantastic actions. It is possible for the historian to commit errors and relate something that has not happened, and for the novelist to insert a rigorously historical deed in the novel. Historicity may change, but illocution remains the same. Since historians declare themselves to be truthful and demand that we believe them, we may criticize and accuse them if they fall into error. For the novelist we must use other criteria.

How do deliberate liars make their utterances? By separating two planes of the language, inverting the judgment on the truth of what is enunciated.

> Lips that maliciously flatter
> are the glaze that coats earthenware.
> He who hates dissimulates with his lips
> while inwardly he plans trickery (Prov. 26.23-24).

King Absalom, the usurper, asks Achitophel and Jusay for advice. Both speak as court counsellors, with authority subordinated to royal approval. Both pursue opposing objectives, and the aim conditions the contents and style of their discourses (2 Sam. 17.1-16). The illocution is similar, but the objective is different. Jusay wants to make a senseless counterproductive plan, convincing and feasible. The biblical narrative informs us of this. It also shows us the acts of a seductress (Prov. 7), and of the mother speaking to her children (Bar. 4.9–5.9).

Ezekiel made his utterances as a prophet using all his resources to make them effective. His hearers listened to his words as beautiful love-songs of no consequence, and undemanding. When these words are fulfilled 'they will realize they had a prophet among them' (Ezek. 33.32-33).

Summary. Illocution is the way of making an utterance, it is implied and not stated. Illocution affects the total meaning of the utterance. Knowledge of illocution ensures correct communication. In the written word, the context often helps us to define illocution.

10. *The Symbol*[11]

The symbol has a primary function in order to know and express themselves. It is difficult to define it, but I may attempt to describe it.

For the symbol to exist, there must be a real sensorial quality. In this reality, there is a fundamental 'plus' present in what is empirical; this empirical cannot be abolished in the interests of that 'plus' of meaning. Should this happen, instead of a symbol there would be an allegory. The sensible reality must be saved because the 'plus' of meaning borne by the symbol is manifested in it. The symbol does not sacrifice its corporeality because transcendency is only manifested in it.

Therefore if the *plus of meaning* is transcendent (divine or human experience), the symbol is an essential instrument for expressing what cannot be said. It is not merely ornamental, but is an instrument for

11. For this theme we consider Paul Ricoeur's contributions, set forth in his extensive bibliography (see bibliography), to be fundamental. See also: L. Alonso Schökel, *Hermenéutica de la palabra*, II (Madrid: Cristiandad, 1987), pp. 118-167; 272-305.

communicating meaning. St Thomas Aquinas in the *Summa Theo-logica*[12] asks if Holy Scripture should use 'metaphors' (=symbols). The conclusion he arrives at is clear: it is important for the Bible to present divine and spiritual realities in corporeal images (*conveniens est sacrae Scripturae divina et spiritualia sub simititudine corporalium tradere*). Also, it is natural for humans to elevate themselves to intelligible reality through sensible things, because all our knowledge has its origin in the senses (*Est autem naturale homini ut per sensibilia ad intelligibilia veniat: quia omnis nostra cognitio a sensu initium habet*).

Symbolic vision is prior to verbal formulation, even though it often emerges in a primarily verbal formula. On the plane of formulation, the symbol is obviously verbal. It is a word or poem that really signifies its object, and in this signifying act it points to another object, not for logical ambiguity but for richness of meaning. It is essential for the word (or poem) to express both its object and, through it, the other, if is to be a real symbol.

'The other' is sometimes grasped in a symbolic vision, which seeks its verbal form, also symbolic; other times the symbolic profundity comes into being precisely in the act of verbal configuration. This happens when we start from the first immediate object; if we start from the mediate, transphenomenal object, the verbal configuration is constituted as the place of the symbolic presence. For example, the poet may pronounce: 'From the rosebush comes the rose', and the rose and nothing else is present in the poetic word. The poet may mention the rose as a term of comparison: 'mas vi la fermosa / de buen continente / la cara plaziente / fresca como rosa' ('but I saw the lovely girl of good bearing and pleasing face, fresh as a rose'; Marqués de Santillana 1398–1458). The poet may give the name of rose to the loved one, to Maria, to baby Jesus: 'Esta reina tan hermosa / ha producido una rosa / tan colorada y hermosa / cual nunca nadie la vio' ('This queen, who is so fair, has brought forth a rose so red and beautiful that none has seen such a one before'; Esteban Zafra). But the poet may pronounce 'rose' referring to the true rose and in it to a revelation of something more: 'the simplicity of perfect roses' (Ruben Darío 1867–1916); 'towards the evening of love, complete, with the rose of fire in our hand' (A. Machado 1875–1939); 'all the roses are the same rose, love, the only rose' (Juan Ramón Jiménez 1881–1958).

12. *Summa Theol.* I, q.1, a9.

The literary symbol is inclusive. It wishes to include the entire object globally, and is thus opposed to the metaphor that is exclusive, limits one aspect and emphasizes it by transformation or synthesis. The metaphor is immanent insofar as it expresses its object, seen in a quality that serves as a link or point of intersection or channel of fusion; while the symbol is transcendent because it encompasses its object and goes beyond its limits towards another. The metaphor has a specific sense, but the symbol is inexhaustible. Since it is global and intuitive, the symbol is diametrically opposed to the literary allegory, which is intensely rational and breaks down the object into pieces for which it seeks articulated correspondence, member by member, in another conventional object; for instance, ages in history and the parts of the body of a statue.

An aspect of the literary symbol that merits special attention is *maturation*. In the author, it means that what in the beginning of their work or poetical activity began as a simple metaphor, matures in profundity until it acquires a symbolic function. In their work, it means that the simple metaphor may be transformed into a symbol: by recurring repetition in a more ample context, or by the action of the literary context, even if there is no repetition. In the reader, it means that what at first was read as a simple metaphor discloses a symbolic quality due to familiarity with an author or a work.

The symbol is deeply rooted in humankind at that point where the corporeal spirit is not yet divided (dichotomized) into body and spirit as contrasting parts. This is why the symbol appeals universally to humans: imagination, intuition and emotion. Those who open themselves contemplatively to the symbol find that it sets up a vibration with them that gets stronger and stronger. The symbol is open and therefore is expansive. In other words, wherever that human structure of body and spirit is united, we would find the capacity to create and understand symbols.

If this is so, the symbol 'creates the person', belongs to the person's constitution, flows from their radical unity as a corporeal spirit or animated body. It may be inhibited or nearly destroyed, but even so continues to exist as a capacity. This explains why the symbol speaks to the average person, because it is common to the whole of humanity in his cultural and historical diversity. It speaks not only to the intellect, but also to emotivity and imagination. People feel interpellated in their entirety. That is why the symbol is important in the integrating forma-tion of the personality. Human beings are frequently moved not only by ideas but also by symbols.[13] Authors of the stature of E. Cassirer and his disciple S. Lange, of K. Rahner, P. Tillich, R. Guardini, advocate the symbolic structure of humankind as an ontological constituent.

Let us remember Guardini's reflections;[14] it is not that we see a face and, by deduction, reach the soul, but it is that the spirit is present and perceptible in the facial expression, the look and the smile. Further-more, if we did not perceive the soul, the most we would see would be a mask; the human face shows only with spiritual configuration. The spirit does not apply previously made and immobile masks, but instead gradually fashions the face.

And we say the same of the body, taking the unity of the human being as a primary fact. It is not that a body is first woven organically to be infused with spirit once it is completed. Rather, the spirit config-urates its body from within, as its paramount manifestation. From within, the spirit places itself in its symbol, which is neither accidental nor conventional. Starting from this first act of symbolizing of the spirit, humans carry out many more, either in concentric circles or in dispersed acts. One of the most important of these is language. I repeat: it is not that the completed spirit adopts a constituted language as extrinsic conventional raiment, but that a spirit seeks and configures its manifestation as sense from within. This is why language is radically a symbol and the presence of sense.

Myths, dreams and art must be placed along the same line. With P. Ricoeur, I say that the myth is not the most radical human manifesta-tion as some think.[15] Without denying its importance, I affirm that it is a derivation of that human capacity to make symbols. The symbol has priority due to the very make up of a human being.

Various classes of symbols can be distinguished: archetypical, cultu-ral, historical and literary.[16] The *archetypical* symbol is that which is

13. A recent work presents this radical human reality to us: M. Girard, *Les symboles dans la Bible: Essai de théologie biblique enracinée dans l'expérience humaine universelle* (Paris: Bellarmin-Cerf, 1991).

14. R. Guardini, *Die Offenbarung: Ihre Wesen und Ilse Formen* (Würzburg: Werkbund, 1940).

15. Paul Ricoeur, *The Conflict of Interpretations* (Evanston, IL: Northwestern University Press, 1974).

16. A good collection of symbols can be found in M. Lurker, *Wörterbuch*

rooted in the spiritual and corporeal human condition. It is also called a 'proto-symbol', so as not to fall into the idea of the archetype as a conceptual abstraction. Archetypical symbols are not to be considered as innate, but they do have a natural matrix that makes them possible: up and down, light and darkness, water and fire, house and road, sleep, mountain... not objects so much as our experiences of them, that begin at the very moment of birth and are deposited in a subliminal form. Although they are carried out in different ways (diverse types of paths), they move without difficulty in time and space. The presence and abundance of these elemental symbols in the Old Testament make biblical poetry contemporary and comprehensible with no special difficulty.

Cultural symbols are those that are characteristic of one or more cultures without being universal. The polar relationship between humans and animals, wild or domesticated, is universal because humans are surrounded by animals. The relationship of hunter and shepherd with animals is cultural. The juridical institution of the '*goel*' (rescue, reclaiming in Exod. 6.6; Lev. 25.25, 48-49; Num. 35.19; Deut. 25.5-6; Isa. 62.12; Jer. 31.11; Ps. 130.8; Job 19.25) is used as a cultural symbol in the Bible.

Historical symbols are those born of a historical or legendary event that acquire symbolical value for the people. The liberation from Egypt and the crossing of the Red Sea have this value for Israel.

Literary symbols are those that arise as literary realities in fiction or creation, and acquire symbolic value (today nobody confuses fiction with falsity). Cain may perhaps be included in this group, the same as Don Quixote or Don Juan. Perhaps in this section would also enter the cosmic or human symbols that have gone through mythical or ancestral elaboration.

As regards historical symbols, it must be made clear that they are very important from a Christian perspective, and explained that we move in a dialectic of event–event and not event–idea. Take the example of Samson, whom a modern author may take as the symbol of the man weakened by love, the strong man defeated by a woman. We shall pay attention to another moment in the life of Samson: his blindness, when he is a blundering man, abandoned by all and the object of general mockery, and who, recovering his strength at a certain moment, demolishes the temple, liberating Israel with his death. We may read

Biblischer Bilder und Symbole (Munich: Kösel, 1973).

this rather poetical story as a symbol (it does not matter what happened in history). This narrative becomes a symbol of another death, that of a ridiculed, despised man who saved all others by dying. Samson symbolizes Christ, not because he represents an idea; Samson dies to save Israel and his death (happening) is for us a symbol of the death of Christ, a new event that reflects the past and is projected to the future.

With respect to literary symbols, it must be said that they do not exist in a pure state, since they always reflect a human experience or condition; but we may conveniently speak of literary symbols.

John stands out among the authors of the New Testament for his symbolic profundity. Paul usually takes juridical symbols, and symbols of human relations; then he reconsiders them with categories that are rabbinical or of Roman law, and makes theology (because the symbol makes one think). All this he always does in order to understand and express the mystery of Christ.

Since the symbol is thought-provoking ('Le symbole donne à penser', Ricoeur), biblical symbology is an essential platform for theological reflection. The intellect may take the symbol and subject it to reflection, and subject that which was global to an articulated discourse. We have seen how a leap is taken from a literary language to a scientific one. It is a legitimate and necessary task. Theology needs its conceptual–technical language to be able to express and refine its achievements. However, reflection on the symbol must avoid an allegorism which annuls it. Moreover, the fact that the symbol provokes thought does not imply it must disappear after reflection. Its expansive force and its richness will always be irreplaceable. And theological reflection will always have to preserve direct contact with the symbolic biblical world, the genuine discourse of the history of salvation where what is transcendent finds expression.

Some think that symbolic language would be updated if a great part of its images were stripped from it; but, on the contrary, it is necessary to return the conceptual expressions of theology to the images from which they came.[17] Reducing biblical expressions to abstract statements may make what we want to update become atemporal. A past human experience, fixed in a literary image, may transmit its communicative force to other periods, while if translated into a conceptual principle, it enters the restricted domain of science.

17. See the example on p. 99.

The symbol is pre-theological or proto-theological in itself. That is to say, purely symbolic biblical language is religious language, not fully theological, since it has not been abstracted. The transfer of one language to another is the consequence of a historical process.

We may say that, in its early days, the Church regarded the prevailing Greek philosophy with mistrust. Stoic ethics was not looked upon unfavourably, but there was certain apprehension directed towards human wisdom in connection with the proclamation of its message. The preachers preferred to speak in biblical language, with which they had been nurtured in the Old Testament, thus creating the New Testament.

The great confluence of two cultures which forged the West was gradually reached. A firm connection was established between Greek philosophy, preferably Platonic, and the biblical medium. The Church thus found a philosophical mould into which to pour its tradition. With the help of Platonism, patristic reflection encompassed languages. This fruitful embrace was imitated in subsequent generations. Faced with problems of heterodoxy posed by theological reflection and Christian living, the Church tried to define and perfect the authentic tradition by using a philosophical language which was free of ambiguities, but direct contact with the Bible was never lost, and symbolical sensibility was kept.

Nevertheless, Platonism took root in such a way that, when Aristotelanism arose forcefully in the West in the thirteenth century, the latter was repeatedly condemned as unsuitable for receiving the Christian message. However, with St Thomas, it was officially accepted and Aristotelian conceptualization, expert in distinguishing and subdistinguishing, marked the ensuing theological method of scholasticism. Following on from this moment, the great danger (into which St Thomas did not fall) was to lose contact with the sacred text, fountainhead of theological study, and fall into the decadent use of *argumentum Scripturae*.

The symbol is part of the life of the Church. In the sixteenth and seventeenth centuries, those of the Church's greatest missionary expansion, arose the pressing problem of inculturation. The Christian religion searches for paths to enter into other cultures and mentalities.

The way of doing this was not unitary, and nearly always erred from an attitude of western superiority. Perhaps the Franciscans in Latin America were those who conserved the most direct relationship with the biblical text, especially with the Gospels, in the form of staged performances.

A good method for this task would be to make the Bible the main instrument of evangelization, taking advantage of its symbolic richness. Observing how those archetypical, cultural and historical symbols are articulated in each mentality—the Bible is filled with them—'cultural transfer' could then be attempted on a common plane, developing the message with the elements and terminology of local culture. Let us take an example: the relation 'favour', common to any people whatsoever, may be the vessel of the biblical *hen* much better than creating a neologism to translate the metaphysical–theological elaboration of *gratia*.

As an important organ of tradition in the Church, liturgy is where the symbolic language that expresses transcendental experience has been best conserved. Liturgy could be the school of initiation to what is symbolic, because many symbols in it are presented in action. It would be wrong to approach liturgy with a purely conceptual reflection. In the liturgy of Holy Saturday night, the experience with fire, light and water should be re-enacted. The Eucharist was a simple meal among friends. The liturgical texts try to exploit the symbolic value of the actions, gathering together and updating biblical expressions. Liturgy is not a mystery because it is unintelligible, but because it attempts to present in symbols what is inexpressible.

At this point, I wish to add some further reflections to all that I have said so far. The insistence on the necessity of immediate contact with the Bible does not aim at denying relationship with theology, which is also necessary. Theology must continue its history, of which it is a debtor, but its contact with the Bible is fundamental if it does not wish to fall again into another neo-scholastic conceptualism.

Why do theologians find it so hard to present the Church as *sponsa Christi*, presented so splendidly in the Bible and discussed by the Fathers of the Church? Or in christology, where the *magister salmanticensis* Friar Luis de León gives us a lesson in this aspect. Leaving temporarily the scholastic method and the Latin of his classes, he wrote an original christology, that could be called symbolic because it consisted in explaining symbols such as Shoot, Mountain, Sheep, Husband, among others, applying them to Christ.

How good it would be for us to take up again the hermeneutics that considers language not only as *ergon* but as *energeia*, as matrix, as a force generating meaning! What stands out among the infirmities of today's exegesis is the aridity of what is symbolic, and the incapacity of the exegetes of both the Old and New Testaments to grasp and develop biblical symbols. There is, however, a minority of authors who raise their voices in protest against this situation and practise a literary model of exegesis.

The discovery of the solar God in the refrain of Psalm 57 (I do not say sun = God but that God is seen in a solar symbol)—'Rise over the heavens, my God, and the earth be filled with thy glory!' (Ps. 57.6)— may motivate us to the contemplation of God at dawn and also, more theologically, to understand the universalism of Christ's resurrection. Likewise, glimpse the *pater familias*, the farmer in John's parable of the vineyard (Jn 5), in the third part of Psalm 65: 'You tend the land, you irrigate it' (Ps. 65.10).

We are not given a grasp of the symbolic potential of the texts by philology alone, nor by an analysis of the sources that gave rise to the text. In spite of this, the symbolic potential remains there for our contemplation and comprehension of the mystery, in short, for our ex/egesis.

Is there anything that constitutes the symbolic structure of beings, our knowledge and in particular, biblical interpretation? The answer for believers is affirmative: the foundation is Christ, as prime symbol. In Christ, the whole of creation subsists and means symbolically; ancient economy and its books subsist in him and express him symbolically.

Christ is the *proto-symbol* of God, the first exteriorization of God. It must be well understood that 'first' is an ontological and not chronological term. God manifesting God's self, coming out of self to show self, configurating from within the place and means of God's presence—that is Christ. Other circles of new symbolic presence are detached from this first exterior, close or immediate circle. Thus, history and creation are symbols of Christ.

If the vine grows, gives fruit and transmutes the elements into juice and wine, it is because Christ is the true vine. If light shines, dawns and illuminates, it is because Christ is light. *Ut intelligas Deum fecisse lucem cum Christus a morituis resurrexit* (St Augustine, *Enarrationes in Psalmos* 47.1).

The external circles must be passed through so as to reach the central one; before the central plenitude of Christ made man on earth, there was the historical wave that already contained him and manifested him symbolically. That historical wave, ancient economy, is the symbol of Christ: events, institutions and people. As they travel along the long road, people illuminated by faith contemplate, see the dawn and rejoice: the symbol begins to fulfil its destiny of manifestation, and is recovered and accepted in their movement. People assisted by the Spirit take the object in their experience and transform it into a word which fixes and symbolically encloses the mysterious reality; there is a second opening of the symbols, and the process of recovery moves and dams them. Those verbal symbols or real symbols open once again to the contemplation of faith, becoming enriched and mature, to the final illumination in which verbal and real symbols are reduced to the centre, Christ. 'Thanks to the mystery of the Word made man, the light of your glory shone before our eyes with renewed splendour, so that knowing God visibly, He may lead us to love of what is invisible' (Preface at Christmas, Roman liturgy).

Christ, the first creature, founds the existence of all creatures, that have consistency in him. Christ, the first symbol, founds the sense of all creatures, who fulfil their symbolic function in him.

Summary. The symbol manifests its transcendency in its corporeality, since in it there is a 'plus' of meaning. There are several types of symbols: archetypical, cultural, historical and literary. The literary symbol is inclusive and can mature. The symbol provokes thought and because of this, the task of conceptualization of the symbol is legitimate and necessary, but reflection must not lead to its disappearance.

Chapter 8

THE TEXT

1. *The Work/Text*

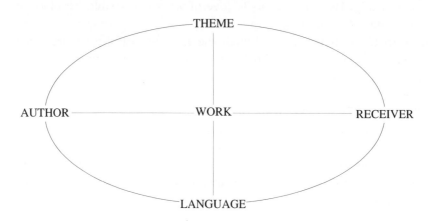

In the centre of the diagram I have placed the work/text, because, in the first and last instance, this is what is of highest concern. The reason for our efforts is to comprehend the text and explain it once comprehended, so that it may be understood. We want to pay attention to a literary text as an ideal total unit and to each of its units of sense. We wish to reflect on the comprehension and explanation of the literary text.

Instead of text we could say work. Text seems a more generic term, specified by adding an article: a text, the text, and so it more or less coincides with the work, which is a concrete, unitary and unique text. A text may be a short proverb, 'Like mother like daughter', 'a chip off the old block', and may be longer, such as the Deuteronomist's history or the book of Job; it may be the Psalter, a psalm, a refrain of a psalm; it may be Peter's discourse at Pentecost or the Acts of the Apostles or Luke–Acts.

When we say 'text', etymology leads us to the world of the weavers, to the loom with its temple and shuttle, weft and warp. *Textum* is the past participle of *texo* (=weave). We may imagine a language as an undefined piece of cloth in which not only two series of perpendicular fibres cross each other, but the fibres also interweave in three dimensions. We cut a part of this available cloth that is language in order to make a suit, dress or habit, tablecloth or bedcover, that is unpretentious or *haute couture*. The advantage of this etymological comparison is that it shows the relationship between the work/text and its language. It makes us see the text as a work of language. St Augustine said: 'So that from this verse [Ps. 133.1] comprehension of the complete fabric of the psalm may come down to us' (*intellectus universae texturae psalmi*).[1]

The term 'work' indicates the result of a task, the completed lasting product; it suggests a closed unit, and embraces its entirety. A text may be the lamentation for Melibea's death, the work is the *Tragicomedia de Calixto y Melibea* (whether simple or compound). In the following pages I shall use both terms, text and work, without insisting on their differences. Most biblical texts are literary works.

2. What Is the Literary Work?[2]

The literary work is not to be identified with its materials nor is it the sum of them. It is not the written text as such, since writing is only a record or notation: the work may subsist in the memory or be recorded on a disc. Neither does it consist in recitation which is multiple, repeated and diverse; recitation or reading is a *reproductive interpretation*. Neither is it the author's experience as such, which is neither simply nor fully objectified, and may surpass the work. Nor is it the experience of the reader or audience, individual or social.

The work consists in a complex verbal system, in a system of structures on different planes, related among themselves. It is a system of significant forms. The record conserves the potential work; this is enacted and exists again with every performance (reading, recitation, stage performance, execution, etc.). The work subsists and is transmitted in a tradition. The work has its own consistency: the form conserves

---

1.   St Augustine, *Enarrationes in Psalmos* 132.1.
2.   Here I resume some ideas already developed in Alonso Schökel, *La palabra inspirada*, pp. 243-66.

the sense. The work is repeatable and wishes to be repeated, but is it inherently changeable?

The example of music may help us to understand. Sheet music is not the musical work, which is a system of sounds. It is not a sonata or concerto, but only its conventional notation. The musical work exists only while it is being performed or interpreted. The same Beethoven sonata is interpreted by many maestros: it is always different, always the same. Whoever knows it recognizes it in each new performance. The expert appreciates a diversity of nuances—some listen to it mentally.

It will be objected that the musical example is not valid because its forms are not significant, or at least it does not articulate meaning. This is true; the musical example is valid for semiotics but not for semantics.

Perhaps this masterly sonnet on books, 'Desde la Torre'of Quevedo (1580–1645), may offer us a more complete, profound and ample vision of the reality of the literary work:

> Withdrawn to the peace of this wilderness,
> in the company of a few learned books,
> I live in conversation with the dead
> and listen to them with my eyes.
>
> If not always understood, always open,
> and either emend or fertilize my thoughts;
> and as silent musical counterpoints
> to the sleep of life, they speak while awake.
>
> Great don Josef! learned print frees
> great souls taken away by death
> from the damage of years.
>
> The hour flees in irrevocable flight;
> but it [time] counts as the best
> that which [is spent] improving us by learning and study.

3. *Semantics and Semiotics*

Semiotics deals with the sign in and of itself and analyses its immanent organization. Semantics considers the work in its signification as a mediator of sense. In a provisional and superficial way, some will distinguish them thus: Semiotics studies what is formal, the system of forms and its immanent relationships. Although it looks at the work from outside, semiotics encloses itself in the work and does not leave it. Semantics deals with the contents, which is what the forms mean.

The distinction between form and contents in this section may help incidentally. In fact, literary form and contents are correlative, mutually implied, and are not understood separately. The entire being of the literary work is semantic and significant; otherwise we would have only 'songs without words'. Forms and their mutual relationships are significant. This is not to deny that purely formal elements may be lodged in the work.

Just as we cannot forget nor dispense with meaning in language forms, neither should we dispense with the reality and function of the work as globally significant. I shall explain it with some principles and examples.

a. *The Work Is a Macrostructure*

Here, I want to communicate that the total unit affects the meaning of its parts, and that we cannot understand the meaning of each part if we do not refer to the totality. The degree may vary without annulling the substance. We find an example as clear as it is significant in Manuel Machado's song to the cities of Andalusia, 'Canto a Andalucía':

> Cádiz salada claridad. Granada
> agua oculta que llora,
> Romana y mora, Córdoba callada,
> Málaga cantaora,
> Almería dorada,
> plateado Jaén, Huelva la orilla
> de las tres carabelas.
> Y Sevilla.

> Cadiz saline clarity. Granada
> hidden weeping water.
> Roman and Moorish, silent Cordova,
> Malaga flamenco singer.
> Golden Almeria,
> silvered Jaen, Huelva the shore
> of the three caravels.
> And Seville.

Is there anything more trivial, more prosaic, more insignificant than a copulative with a toponym? In the structure of these verses, the insignificant becomes very significant. Every city has its poetic definition; for Seville, its name is sufficient. Paraphrasing: 'Seville! Enough said!' In a second reading, we listen to the entwining of rhymes that interlace the cities: Salada-Granada-callada-dorada (plateado); llora-mora-can-taora; separately, with 'orilla' at the return of Columbus's mythical voyage, Sevilla. Then, after Seville? Full stop.

A sentence is a microstructure. What is the meaning of 'falling'? It is the gerund of the verb 'to fall'. But what does it mean? It depends on the sentence in which it is found: 'Night is falling'. That 'fall' is not the same as that of a fly into the soup, that of soldiers in combat, the 'uniformly accelerated fall of bodies in space'. And what does the sentence in itself mean? It depends on its components: 'night', noun without an article; 'is falling', progressive form. Does it signify nothing more? Far more as part of Antonio Machado's poem 'Yo voy soñando caminos... La noche cayendo está' (I go along dreaming of paths... The night is falling). The complete poem is the macrostructure: its meaning depends on all the verses together and the meaning of each verse depends on the whole poem.

A verse-by-verse exegesis runs the risk of losing the whole unit or macrostructure from sight. We search for the meaning of each sentence thinking, perhaps, that, as a mere addition at the end, the meaning of the whole will emerge. This is not so. We link each element to its referent—its exterior object, without first paying attention to its connections within the poem and its function in the literary unit, but a sentence is not to be reduced to a list of words in a dictionary, and a poem is not to be reduced to a list of succesive sentences.

The study of the so-called 'redaction' of the Gospels systematically applies the principle of the whole unit that affects each part. Recent studies of 'narratology' also recognize this principle in the Old Testament.

b. *The Work Creates its Own Universe*

The literary work transposes and globally transforms a complex human experience, creating its own universe in the process. Just as the metaphor displaces the name and takes a detour to point out a new aspect of its object, so the poem displaces the realistic chronicle and neutral reproduction so as to produce a complex that manifests a new sense of reality. The poem or story is like a macro-metaphor.

An invasion of locusts in an agricultural country may naturally be described in zoological terms (migrating *orthoptera*) and botanical terms. It may be described by a poet with moderate realism in a couple of accurate stichs:

It reduces the fig trees to splinters;
it peels, strips off the bark so that
the branches turn white (Joel 1.7).

The plague may also be imaginatively transformed into a swift, merciless cavalry assault (the locust is 'cavallete' in Italian):

In appearance like horses, like cavalry they charge
they bound over the peaks, with a din like chariots (Joel 2.4-5).

The earth ahead is a garden,
behind, it is a desolate steppe (Joel 2.3).

The entire poem (Joel 2.1-11) must be read, allowing oneself to be transported by the imagination to a vision that is coherent, audacious and impressive. The 'scientific' description does not have the same effect, because it has a different function.

The literary work creates a universe of sense that it projects before me, or invites me to enter. 'The novel does not thematize an idea as philosophy does, but makes it exist before us like a thing.'[3] It is like Jeremiah, who sees the milk boil over and flow from the tilted pot and in it sees armies spreading themselves and covering the whole territory (Jer. 1.13-14). It is like Ezekiel, called to enter and act in his vision of the dry bones (Ezek. 37.1-14). It is like the dreamer who enters the happening woven by his uninhibited fantasy.

Let us test this concept with an Italian poem that is not famous, but still very apt for what we need. First, let us adopt an attitude of imaginative contemplation, softly vibrating with emotion: a gentle snowfall, an old woman rocking a cradle and singing, a crying baby who gradually falls asleep, the snow that continues falling. We must leave it in Italian because the quality of the style is one factor of the sense:[4]

Lenta la neve, fiocca, fiocca, fiocca.
Senti; Una zana dondola pian piano.
Un bimbo piange, il piccol dito in bocca;
canta una vecchia, il mento nella mano.
La vecchia canta: 'Intorno al tuo lettino
c'è rosa e gigli; tutto un bel giardino'.

---

3. M. Merleau-Ponty, *Sens et non sens*, p. 51 (quoted in Ray, *Literary Meaning*, p. 18).

4. *Fioccare* = fall; *zana* = wicker cradle; *dondola* = rocks; *piano* = slowly; *c'è* = there is.

Nel bel giardino il bimbo s'addormenta.
La neve fiocca lenta, lenta, lenta...

Snowflakes are falling, falling, falling.
Listen: a cradle rocks slowly, slowly.
A baby cries, his little thumb in his mouth;
an old woman sings, her chin in her hand.
The old woman sings: 'Around your little bed
there are roses and lilies, a whole beautiful garden'.
In the beautiful garden the baby falls asleep.
The snowflakes fall gently, gently, gently.

As information, the poem offers very little (it is anonymous); as an emotive evocation, the poem is attractive. Our eyes rest on details: his thumb in his mouth, her chin in her hand; we feel the movement in counterpoint of the snow and the cradle; we hear the crying and the singing until the latter prevails. We are present at the scene, we enter as spectators, we feel deep emotion. There is something else explicit in the poem: with her song, the old woman has musically conjured up 'a garden of roses and lilies'; the baby enters that garden and goes to sleep in it. Similarly, we enter the poem and share its reality and its meaning. What we say about the poem is also valid for the tale, but not for the purely informative exposition.

4. *The Work: A Closed World?*

We are not enclosed in the work, because we are not speaking of the genre of fantasy, science-fiction, whose universes exist only in the imagination of the author and reader. It is true that fantastic literature has multiple links with reality, links that serve to draw away from it and supplant it. It is also true that fantastic literature may provide a healthy exercise for our imagination, too atrophied by cultural laziness. However, we are not dealing with that here. We have adduced the example of fantastic literature so as to focus the problem for its similarity. Is the poetic narrative universe a world I shut myself into with other readers and the author? A world of forms and relationships that share a mutual basis and are justified by their immanent coherence?

The literary work, the biblical work (without excluding the Apocalypse—theology-fiction), is a system of significant forms and a significant macroform. The movement from semiotics to semantics is interesting. We should neither put the work aside nor wall ourselves up within it. The key lies in recognizing the significant forms. If I were dealing with pure forms, the study would fall into formalism; but if the form in literature creates sense, the study is legitimate and necessary.

Summary. The literary work is a work of language which consists in a complex system of significant forms. The work has its own consistency, is repeatable and wishes to be repeated. The work is a macrostructure: the entire unit affects the sense of its parts, and we cannot understand the sense of each part unless we refer to the entirety. The work creates its own universe which we are invited to enter.

5. *The Truth of Literature*

I approach this theme from the angle of the autonomy and mediation of the literary work.[5]

We have briefly discussed the preoccupation, almost obsession, for the inerrancy of a treatise of inspiration focused on judgment: false judgment is impossible in a Bible inspired by God. The expression 'inerrancy' is negative but it indicates a positive quality, 'truth'.

Doubtlessly the Bible, especially the New Testament and within it the epistles in particular, contains numerous enunciations or judgments which claim the indisputable quality of being true:

> The Lord will bring to light the hidden things of darkness
> and will make manifest the intentions of the hearts:
> then every man shall receive his praise from God (1 Cor. 4.5).

Paul is conscious here of proposing true teaching, in its entirety and in its singular propositions. They are not evident in themselves, and are not accompanied with demonstration; the believer receives them as truth guaranteed by the Spirit. They do not pose in principle a hermeneutical problem. The problem lies in literary texts, particularly in narrative and poetry. We will deal with the question in two steps: the truth of the metaphor (and in general of the image) and the truth of the literary work (macrostructure).

a. *The Rule of Metaphor* [6]
Is the metaphor false, ornamental, true? Taken literally, a metaphoric sentence is false: 'Pull down that temple...' (he referred to the temple

---

5. This theme has been dealt with from another perspective in Alonso Schökel, *La palabra inspirada*, pp. 297-317.

6. Cf. P. Ricoeur, *La métaphore vive* (Paris: Seuil, 1969).

of his body)... 'I am the way...', 'I am the light of the world...', 'the water I shall give him will become in him a spring that gushes forth giving eternal life...' (John). 'The Lord will dawn on you... a multi-tude of camels will swamp you... Who are those who fly like clouds, like doves to the dovecote? They are ships coming to me' (Isa. 60). 'Nineveh is a reservoir whose water is leaking away' (Nah. 2). Here the distinction between comparison and metaphor does not matter much. Taken literally they are false, but taken literally they are no longer metaphors.

Is the metaphor simply ornamental? Let us say instead that it is something unnecessary and added to make things attractive: cream on the cake, a golden button without a buttonhole, moulding that conceals. There are metaphors like these, redundant and dispensable for sense; they could be dismissed with a small indemnity for their trouble. Such metaphors cannot be the measure of authentically substantial ones, mediators of sense.

Although neither inspired nor sublime, the authentic metaphor (and image) has a cognitive function. It aims at revealing an aspect of the object that would otherwise remain hidden or be unreachable, or would not strike the reader. When the worshipper says he is surrounded by a pack of dogs (Ps. 22), he wants to reveal his enemies' ferocity. When he says he will not stumble, he reveals life and conduct as a way or pilgrimage. On relating two entities, ripe fig and threatened city, the metaphor makes the fig reveal an aspect of the city that will soon sur-render. 'To he who longs for death, which does not come, and digs to search for it more than if it were a treasure' (Job 3.21). Active yearning on the part of he who searches to unearth a hidden treasure in order to be buried himself, because underground death, mistress of the obscure realm of the dead, is a treasure that must be reached so that it will reach me. People 'live in houses of clay with mud foundations, and they collapse between dawn and sunset' (4.19-20): humanity moulded in clay, inhabitant of a body of fragile adobe disintegrated by water; from birth to death elapses only one day from dawn to sunset. 'The arrows of the Almighty are thrust into me and I feel how I absorb their poison. God's terrors have been deployed against me' (6.4). With this imagina-tive language, the author of the book of Job explores an entire continent of human existence and is presenting it to readers 'forever and ever'. Let no one dare to accuse this brilliant writer of treating a tremendous theme with formal play and of concealing the pathetic truth of the problem with an accidental decor.

b. *The Statute of the Literary Work*
Now that the ground is prepared with the observation of the truth of the metaphor (or image), we may go more deeply into observation of the macro-metaphor which is the literary work.

I repeat that, in the Old Testament, and even more in the New Testament, are found doctrinal works that, if more difficult to understand, are easier to justify for their truth. The epistle to the Romans is an eminently doctrinal tract. It proposes and develops a coherent doctrine, combining everyday, technical and literary language. What must not be forgotten is that, being a unitary work, the whole affects the sense of the parts and, consequently, each part must be understood in the context of the entire organism. Exegetes practise this by mutual agreement. Doctrinal texts also contain many propositions presented as true; and, if they are unitary, they develop a conception that may be formulated in a proposition, a sort of title, presented as a true one.

The condition of literary texts, both *narrative* and *poetic*, is different. Are they themselves propositions or do they contain them? Should those presented as grammatical propositions be considered as true logical propositions? Some critics have pronounced a summary judgment: poets neither affirm nor deny, their works are neither true nor false, they should not not aspire to be taken seriously. As Ezekiel's fellow countrymen said to him in Babylon: 'Singer of love songs with a good voice, and a good player' (Ezek. 33.33). I now treat the questions which distinguish between narrative and poetry in greater depth (even though the boundaries are artificial and fluid).

1. *The narrative.* The historical narrative makes its truth consist in its correspondence with events that happened and exactly as they happened. We usually call that truth 'historicity'. All the sense of the event has happened, and all the truth of the narrator is recording it so as to inform us thereof. However, the authentic historian looks for meaning behind the pure event, and tries to explain it by its causes, effects, circumstances and intentions. All of this aspires to a second truth, that of interpretation, and naturally thence to the logical truth of propositions. Neutral chronicles and historiography still exhibit their truth as doctrinal works do, the difference is that they relate and explain individual deeds instead of proposing a general doctrine.

Narrative fiction covers a range of types: pure fiction, historical novels with real-life characters, history with fictitious characters, legend, parable, fantastic stories and so on. Grammatically, fiction proceeds like historical accounts; intentionally, it does not aim at recording events that did happen. Measured with the yardstick of historicity, narrative fiction is false. Taken as it is, it has its truth.[7]

A special point must be made of this, because there are still many who identify fiction with falsity, and therefore do not want to admit it in the Bible. All fundamentalism is built on the sand of this fallacy. The parables of the Gospels could be mentioned in order to demonstrate the truth of fiction. The truth of fiction may be of two basic types. The fictitious story sometimes covers and disguises a historical happening; perhaps it leaves holes or rents where the happening is visible, or through which the reader can take a look. Judith's story is not historical, but it allows glimpses into historical facts, besides offering an interpretation of sense. 'The only way fiction has of expressing the world is pointing at it in stories.'[8] At other times, its truth is not singular or individual, but consists instead in the exploration and presentation of aspects of the human condition. This is so in great novels and, to a certain extent, also in unpretentious ones. We may call it 'generalization'. The author observes, extracts, combines, invents, produces an individual case—the more intensely individual the better—in that case, it reveals a general reality. This concerns the entire work, and also its elements, and may even be appreciated in some sentences.

In his book *El invierno en Lisboa*, Muñoz Molina uses the comparison to generalize:

> 'It was like suddenly awakening,' said Biralbo, 'like when you've fallen asleep at midday and you wake up at nightfall and you don't recognize the light neither do you know where you are nor who you are. It happens to the sick in hospital'.[9]

Other times he pigeon-holes the fact in a category (he generalizes):

> In his look I observed the stupor of one who has spent many hours alone.

7.   Cf. M. Sternberg, *The Poetics of Biblical Narrative: Ideological Literature and the Drama of Reading* (Bloomington, IN: Indiana University Press, 1985).

8.   Merleau-Ponty, *Sens et non sens*, p. 55.

9.   Antonio Muñoz Molina, *El invierno en Lisboa* (Barcelona: Seix Barral, 1987).

2. *Narrative and poetry*. Let us take up the accusation again, valid for both poetry and narrative: the poets neither affirm nor deny, their works are neither true nor false. In order to respond to this accusation, we must confront its presupposition. According to Aristotle and all scholasticism after him, truth resides in the proposition or enunciation, not in simple intellectual apprehension or perception. If I say 'paper', I say neither truth nor falsehood; all I do is pronounce the name of an object in a language. In German it would be 'Papier', in Italian 'carta': the name is conventional and does not coincide, although the concept does. But none claims the attribute of truth exclusively for itself. Truth/falsity begin when I affirm: 'The paper is white.' It is in this way that the poets neither affirm nor deny, therefore they do not belong to this category.

> So continue, knife, continue
> flying, wounding. Some day
> yellow(ing) time will land
> on my photograph.[10]

Does a knife fly? Is that 'knife' a real knife? Does time have colour? Does time lie on a flat object? Neither true nor false; typical of poets!

> Justice and Peace kiss each other;
> Fidelity flows from the earth
> and Justice leans out from heaven (Ps. 85.11-12).

Are Justice and Peace two friends who kiss each other when they meet? Is Justice an inquisitive neighbour who leans out from a heavenly window? Although the modern poem and the biblical one are different, neither of them comes into the category of true or false propositions. Let us make the test with two other fantastic pieces.

> The Lord halts and the earth trembles,
> he casts a glance and disperses the nations.
> The old mountains crumble,
> the primordial hills and the primordial orbits
> prostate themselves before him...
> You strip and alert your bow,
> you fill your quiver with arrows,
> you split the earth with torrents...
> You tread on the sea with your horses
> and the immensity of the waters boils (Hab. 3.6, 9, 15).

10. Miguel Hernández (1910–42), 'El rayo que no cesa'.

The pontiff goes towards the East.
Is he going to find the golden barque
where in the brightness of dawn
King January comes in triumph?
December's quiver has already been emptied
by the Archer's bow.
On the shore of eternity's mysterious abyss
immense Sagitarius tirelessly draws his bow;
he is sustained by the icy Pole, crowned by white winter
and his loins are covered with the blue fleece of the sea
(Rubén Darío, *Año Nuevo*).

The two poems have a certain kinship because they belong to the realm of imagination. We do not pose the question of truth or falsehood to the Nicaraguan poet; Habakkuk's poem is presented as 'God's word': does he also evade the question?

6. *Logical and Ontological Truth*[11]

I reply to the previous question with a basic distinction. Aristotle spoke of logical truth which consists in dividing to recompose. He divides into subject and predicate and joins them with the conjunction or in the proposition, 'the paper is white'. However, there is another truth previous to logical truth, an essential foundation of it. It is the truth of the existing being which manifests itself with its presence and is apprehended by the intellect. We may call this truth ontological (some prefer a tripartite division: logical of proposition, ontical of the entity, ontological of the being). In a simple act of my intellect, which may be called intuition, I apprehend my 'white-paper' object; that intuition splits it into two pieces 'white'/'paper', which I then join with the copula 'is'. The scholastics said profoundly: '*ens est verum*' (being is true); and they referred to that fundamental condition. That 'unveiling' of the entity in its presence before human intellect is its truth, which is ontological, its basis and prior to logic.

The truth of literary narrative and of poetry belongs to this second type. The writers neither affirm nor deny: they place a portion of the being in front of the intellect, and the readers apprehend it directly. The being, a snippet of life or human experience, is present before the readers, and the readers are present before the text. But how do beings

11. L. Lerner's contribution is important in this theme, *The Truest Poetry: An Essay on the Question: What Is Literature?* (New York: Horizon Press, 1964).

present themselves in the literary work? By re-presentation, as, for example, Abraham bargaining with God like a merchant: he is not alive, he is not before me; he is present in the text by re-presentation (Gen. 18.23-33). The daughter of Jephthah, receiving her victorious father with tambourines, weeping over her thwarted motherhood through the mountains: she is neither our fellow countrywoman nor our contemporary: she is present only on that poignant page in the Bible (Judg. 12.34-39). And the woman clad in sunshine, treading on the moon, crowned with a constellation of stars? There she is in the text, revealing a mystery of fruitful sorrow, persecution and victory as an image on the celestial screen (Rev. 12.1). Sartre said: 'As in the theatre, when we read, we enter the presence of a world... Reading a novel is taking an attitude similar to that of the spectator.'[12]

Within the work as a macrostructure may be lodged logical propositions subject to the quality of being true or false.

7. The Truth of Lyric

The truth of lyric does not consist in communicating what the author feels—an analogical 'historicity' like that of an autobiography. Rather, the truth of the author is called sincerity, and may be found in poetry of the romantic type.

In the biblical lyric of the psalms, the poet usually interposes the 'I' of the poem. If we call the author 'the psalmist', we shall call the 'I' who says the prayers 'the worshipper'. A perfectly healthy poet writes a supplication for a sick man (Ps. 38), for a dying man (Ps. 88), the libretto for a celebration with soloist and chorus (Ps. 118). The book of Job combines lyric and drama enclosed within a narrative framework. Some commentators probe the text in search of a proposition that will give an answer to the problem. For them, it does not suffice to contemplate a person who suffers without reason, who wants to discuss the injustice of their torment with God, and finally tells us they have seen God: 'I had only heard of you; now my eyes have beheld you' (Job 42.5). He had heard many propositions, perhaps pro and contra, but now he stands before a satisfying presence.

The procedure of generalization is also practised in lyric. The person at prayer arises from personal experience to the experience shared by

12. J.-P. Sartre, quoted in Ray, *Literary Meaning*, p. 18.

all or by many. Their case is true as an individual of a species; in their case a common experience is revealed.

There are many types of lyric in the Bible:[13] political satire, social denunciation, songs of hope, debates, woes, blessings. Each one has its truth, not always in the form of propositions. Even grammatical propositions are not always logical statements. The theme of illocution that we have already discussed helps us to complete this succinct exposition.

Summary. The metaphor has a cognitive function. Fiction is not the same as falsity. The truth of the literary narrative and of poetry belong to the sphere of ontological truth. The being is presented in the literary work by re-presentation.

8. *Text Tradition*

a. *Tradition: Vital Medium of the Text*

The text is born on the author's horizon, but does it remain bound forever to its historical–vital horizon without breaking the umbilical cord that gave it the possibility of existing? If we compare the text with a nautical vessel, must it remain moored to the jetty in port for all of its life? By no means. The text should be capable of navigating, otherwise it will never be modern. This capability of the text to 'draw away' is one of the essential qualities of the literary work; this is one of the functions of having it written. That sailing of the text requires a medium, a sea where it may develop its navigation. This medium that sustains the text and in which the text leaves its wake is tradition. This is a fact common to any text.

In the case of the Bible, tradition acquires a normative, charismatically particular character. All texts live, carried by tradition, like water that sustains the vessel and makes it advance. Hermeneutically, this aspect is so essential that we could establish the equation text = text+ tradition: for a text is always *textus traditus*. If tradition is broken, comprehension is made extremely difficult. Why is it so arduous for us to read the Greek or Latin classics today? Because they no longer constitute the *humus* of humanistic and literary education.

---

13. Cf. L. Alonso Schökel, *Antología de poesía bíblica hebrea* (Zaragoza: Delegación de catequesis, 1992).

b. *The Dialectic Process of Reciprocity*

Tradition is a medium necessary for the intelligibility and life of the text. A text lives and continues to live in tradition; without it, the text dies. Tradition enters a dialectic process of reciprocity with the text in such a way that it is capable of conditioning its intelligence and comprehension. Not only does tradition sustain the text, but it also becomes an unavoidable horizon of comprehension of the text. I repeat that it is a reciprocally dialectical process. It is not enough to say that a text tradition is sufficient just the moment I have it in front of me, because, in tradition, we find both the text and the movement which has brought it to us. The immediate relationship with the text is irreplaceable, although, in reading and interpretation, tradition is present as a condition of possibility and the shaping of its intelligence. Let us see it in a diagram:

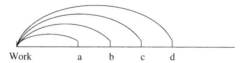

Work   a   b   c   d

Every historical moment (a, b, c, d...) is bound to tradition (horizontal line) and to text (arch). This is fundamental. If I find myself in 'd' I must have direct contact with the 'Work', but I continue to remain behind 'a–b–c' on the line of tradition that both conditions and makes understanding possible for me.

The Bible is the determining factor of what Christians are. What I am now, a Christian of the twentieth century, has also been determined by the Bible. The community reads the gospel and the gospel shapes the community. So I, the reader, am part of the Bible, the result of the biblical text, and as such I read it. Familiarity, congeniality and reception exist between both. I am not a neutral reader. I do not read the Bible as an archaeological curiosity or as a simple object of study. If I read it and want to understand it in depth, I must allow it to shape and mould me. It is a living text, and its communication of meaning exercises an influence on life. It not only communicates knowledge but is a live and vivifying force. Whoever reads it is invigorated by its force and gradually becomes a Christian. There is a mutual involvement of living and comprehending in a dialectic of reciprocity between the text and its tradition.

c. *Live Tradition: Transmission of Life*

Transmission of the text is a vital and vivifying act since, as in human life, when life is given, the capacity for transmitting it is also communicated. In this case, the transmitting subject is the whole Church and each one of its members. If we think of the time factor, we observe that it is a generational act. The first community receives the gospel; with that generation, the writing of the gospel is more or less completed. The second generation receives the gospel together with the comprehension of it transmitted by the first. The third receives the text with the received and also matured comprehension… and so on. Tradition cannot be conceived as an unchangeable block, but as a vital dynamic reality. The increasing comprehension that a generation has of the text becomes a horizon for itself and for successive generations.

d. *In the Mystery of the Spirit*

The Holy Spirit is a decisive factor in the tradition of the biblical text. Here believers detach themselves from the common manner of the cultural transmission of any text. In the act of communicating meaning, the text transmits Spirit.

When I read and seek comprehension of the text, the Spirit helps and enlightens me. The Fathers of the Church said that the Bible must be read with the same Spirit with which it was written. In other words, it must be read on the horizon of the Spirit who inspired it, so as to be in tune with it. The Spirit is, at the same time, a guarantee; there is diversity of generations, but a sole Spirit as a constitutive factor of the text and its tradition.

Therefore, defining or clarifying a word, a phrase or a concept, obscured by centuries does not imply having reached the sense. It is true that philology serves and obliges us, but *philology* does not exhaust sense; no less important is the horizon of each moment illuminated in this case by the Spirit. This is because, although closed within itself, the text always remains open to us.

Authors write on their horizons, where many things are obvious for them. Being obvious, they are not explicitly reflected in the text; but this does not mean that they cease to have their influence on the text. I, the reader, can investigate that horizon and thematize and explain that influence that is not obvious to me.

If I read the Epistle to the Galatians I may use the Epistle to the Romans to frame the problem of the former. Furthermore the *Corpus*

Paulinum gives me elements that help me to understand a specific text. Even if in a particular text there are not explicit cross-references, the influence of the general context is present, for me to discover. It may also happen that an author has a brilliant intuition (St Augustine may be a genuine exponent of this type of author), but he does not develop it. It will be the concern of future generations to work out the potential which lies there.

The reader, then, may go further than what the author formulated or intended. History may produce moments, situations, signs, that make possible the display of the author's intuitions. And the inverse: in history itself, such intuitions (for example, the theme of the 'slave's liberty' in Paul) have acted as a ferment contributing to events that the author never even imagined. In the end, these events will become revealing factors of the potential sense of such intuitions.

How is this dynamic possible? By means of the expansive force of the symbol. Creators of a symbol may not grasp all its force, or may feel that the symbol 'gets away' from them once created. Coming generations will have to discover the force with which it is imbued. This dynamic is also possibly due to the force of the Spirit who, we must not forget, directs that history in which the text lives and grows. It is up to each generation to perceive its vivifying breath in the events of each day.

Scripture lies in the sphere of mystery and will therefore never be exhausted. The words of Jesus in John's Gospel are thus shown to be true: 'When the Spirit of truth comes, he will guide you into all the truth, for he will not speak on his own authority, but will speak only what he hears, and he will make known to you what is to come' (Jn 16.13). We thus understand the interest of the Second Vatican Council in presenting tradition not as a static block to be conserved and transmitted intact, but as a dynamic dialectical reality, transmitting life.

e. *The Poles of Tradition*

With tradition seen as a living reality in the transmitting subject, in the act of transmission, in what has been transmitted and in the medium of transmission, it is impossible to understand it as a purely conservative force. Conservation is only one pole of tradition; the other is progress. The joint action of the two poles creates the unified force field of tradition. Whoever artificially isolates one of the poles deforms reality, and is thus not even capable of explaining the artificially isolated pole.

If tradition looks at its beginnings, its attitude is one of fidelity and continuity: it thus maintains its own identity, connected with the given or imposed commencement. If it looks at its end, its attitude is one of tendency and tension: it thus conserves its dynamism, its dissatisfaction with what is incomplete, and it lives in hope.

However, a complementary affirmation must be added. The beginning is also a dynamic impulse, insofar as the being is given as a task, and the reality given is alive and dynamic. Analogously the eschatologic tendency demands conservation and fidelity because only in it can plenitude be approached and reached.

Tradition is a condition of possibility and a conditioning of what is transmitted—in this case, the biblical text. However, it may go astray to the point of going against the text, as in the case of an aberrant or falsifying tradition. It may also become rigid, dogmatic and closed, and not progress as it should, as in the case of a paralysing tradition. It may also happen that, due to the plurality of interpretations admitted by the symbol, tradition branches off into diverse interpretations, all of them possible, but not all plausible.

Tradition thus makes text possible but also endangers it. With the knowledge of possible risks, confirmed by history, it is wiser to allow a degree of restraint which is controlled in the first instance by the text itself. In the case of ambiguous tradition, it is necessary to resort to a normative or authoritative interpretation.

It must be kept in mind that humans' memory does not go back further than a century, and, because of this, we may believe that tradition begins there. We may consider failures, ruptures and deviations as 'tradition', and we may not even feel it necessary to make recourse to previous moments in the tradition, and far less to the text itself. A historical glance may show us that they are perhaps merely 'abberrant' or 'paralysing' traditions. Today, for example, we are nearer to genuine biblical tradition than last century because, conscious of the rupture it suffered in the long Protestant controversy, we have again taken up a moment of the tradition more authentic than that offered to us by the generations that immediately preceded ours.

Summary. Tradition is the medium necessary to understand the text. Tradition enters a dialectical process of reciprocity with the text: both preserving it and conditioning its understanding. For the biblical text, the Holy Spirit is a decisive factor in tradition. Tradition is developed between two poles: conservation and progress.

9. *The Development of Sense: Biblical Examples*

Important texts frequently contain an overflowing wealth of sense. The margins surpassed by the volume of sense are mutually linked, but I distinguish between them to make the explanation clear. Following the image, sense may overflow at the margin of the author, or at that of the reader.

(1) The original hearers to whom the message is immediately directed are, for example, the exiled Jews for Ezekiel, the disciples for Jesus. Although this is obvious and universally accepted, it is advisable to pause at the fact, considering that the hearers are an integrating factor of the complex act of communication, and that pragmatics tries to go back to that original moment of communication.

At times, the author attempts to surpass the readers' capacity of comprehension. The motives may be diverse, but the result is the same. The speaker has a superior doctrine to propose: 'If you do not believe when I speak to you of earthly things, how are you going to believe when I speak to you of heavenly things?' (Jn 3.13, Jesus to Nicodemus); in the preceding dialogue, John has just demonstrated the incapacity of Nicodemus to follow the discourse of Jesus.

The difficulty may lie in the proposed doctrine or the hearers' situation, be it culpable or not. 'You will say my words to them whether they listen to you or not' (Ezek. 2.7): the listening in question is equivalent to understanding Ezekiel's words in their true sense, as a prophecy, and not as a recital of songs (Ezek. 33.32).

An extreme case is that of the parable of which Mark says: 'To you it is given to know the mystery of the kingdom of God, but to them that are outside, all things are done in parables; that seeing they may see and not perceive, and hearing they may hear and not understand' (Mk 4.11-12). Because of their adverse attitude of mind, they do not understand the true sense of the parables.

Another deliberate case is an *interlocutor's irony*. The interlocutor pronounces words with a double meaning, knowing full well that the other person is going to understand them differently because of their attitude of mind. Such is the masterly piece of irony that is the dialogue between Judith and Holofernes. The vanity of the invincible general and the desire of the lustful male take Judith's words in a sense that corresponds to the text, but not to her significant intention: but it does correspond to her attempt to confound the enemy:

> God sends me to perform a feat with you that will amaze all who hear of it (11.16).

> I swear, your Highness! I will not consume the provisions I have brought before the Lord carries out his plan through me (12.4).

> It will be a happy memory for me until the day I die ... Today is the greatest day of all my life (12.14, 18)

Communication sometimes surpasses the hearers *without the author intending it*, and even against the author's will. Paul realizes this, and makes an effort to adapt himself to the childlike intelligence of his faithful Corinthians; but then he continues with difficult doctrine:

> Brethren, I could not speak to you as spiritual men but as weak ones, as children in Christ. I nourished you with milk, not food, because you were not able to eat as yet. But neither are you now because you still follow your base instincts.
> Have you forgotten that you are the temple of God and that the Spirit of God dwells in you? (1 Cor. 3.1-3, 16)

On other occasions, *the message surpasses the hearers* at first, but it is given so that they may understand it later in the light of events. There is the case of Ezekiel: 'But when they are fulfilled, and they are about to be fulfilled, they will realize they had a prophet among them' (Ezek. 33.33).

Jesus said to Peter: 'What I am doing you do not understand now, but you will understand later' (Jn 13.7). The repeated announcements of the Passion belong to the same type. Let us listen to Luke's version of the second announcement: 'But they did not understand that language; it was so obscure for them that they did not understand the sense, but they were afraid to ask him about it' (Lk. 9.45; Mk 9.32).

(2) No difficult problem arises if the sense of the text surpasses the capacity of the hearer or the reader. Greater difficulty is found when the sense surpasses the author's comprehension.

Let us begin with an analogy taken from narrative art. The narrator or playwright sometimes makes a character say things that, by virtue of the context, go beyond the comprehension of the speaker, but not of the reader/spectator. This is Sophoclean dramatic irony (modelled on King Oedipus).

In Tobit, the angel Gabriel introduces himself as 'an Israelite': 'I am Azarias, the son of the older Ananias'; but neither father nor son know he is an angel. The whole situation is a happy ambiguity, in which some of Tobit's sentences say more than he imagines:

> Welcome, man, you are of good stock! (5.12)

> Son, may his angel accompany you with his protection (5.17).

> Woman, do not torment yourself nor worry over him because a good angel will accompany him, give him a happy journey and bring him back safe and sound (5.22).

Tobit is the character who communicates with his son, his wife and the stranger. The four of them are in a single situation, sharing many religious ideas. There is someone else outside (the author) who makes him speak, giving a different significance to his words. This is an interesting pattern: situation, characters and external author.

Now let us apply the pattern to other cases. On a purely human level in a complex situation, and by the light of one's limited knowledge thereof, one makes an affirmation of limited significance. If the complex situation is known better, or, if after some time the speaker develops their ideas and perhaps resolves the situation, that person is found to have said more than they knew. The sense of the statement went beyond what they wanted to say, changing or twisting the sense of the original utterance.

There is also, however, the level of divine action, that is, when God (the Spirit) holds the position of the external or superior author. For example, a high priest advises the rulers of the need to sacrifice a person so as to save the rest of the people from a great danger, perhaps because that person is increasing the peril. What the priest wants to say and aims at with the advice are clear, but, by God's disposition, the sense of the words surpass the priests intention:

> One of them, Caiphas, who was the high priest that year, said to them: 'You know nothing, you do not consider that it is expedient for you that one man should die for the people rather than that the whole nation should perish.' He did not speak this of himself; but being the high priest that year, he prophesied that Jesus was going to die for the nation; and not only for the nation, but to gather together the children of God that were dispersed (Jn 11.49-51).

According to the pattern, other factors may make the author say more than is known or intended. An eminent case is Ezekiel. He creates a magnificent symbol of the triumph of life over death, by virtue of the Spirit, unaware of what he has created; then, enclosed in his horizon, he offers a narrow interpretation of his inspired vision (Ezek. 37). When Paul affirms that there is no difference between 'Jew and Greek, slave and freeman, man and woman' (Gal. 3.28; cf. Col. 3.11), is he conscious of the reach of his affirmation?

There are also cases in which the author seems to glimpse something beyond the beliefs he shares with his people. The Israelites did not believe in life after death; however, three psalmists pronounce these words:

> For you will not abandon me to Sheol
> your faithful servant to see the pit.
>> you will fill me with joy in your presence,
>> with eternal happiness on your right (Ps. 16.19).
>
>> But God will ransom my life
> And take me from the power of Sheol (Ps. 49.16).
>
>> But I shall always be with you,
>> you will seize my right hand.
>> You lead me according to your plans,
> you take me to a glorious destiny (Ps. 73.23-24).

In these examples, the sense that overflows is the difference between knowing with certainty or clarity and glimpsing or surmizing. The result is that the words transcend the lucid consciousness of the authors.

To these are added many cases in which the sense of the text is so ample that it remains open, even though the author's mind has imposed narrow limits on it. With these we pass on to the third section.

(3) We usually consider the text as an enclosure or precinct. With their intention, the author delimits one of the many possible meanings of a word and excludes the others: the word becomes univocal, unambiguous. With their intention, among the diverse values of the sentence the author defines whether it is interrogative or conditional or ironical: again, the sentence becomes univocal and unambiguous. The author thus marks out boundaries, raises separating walls, so that the sense of the work may be a closed garden: univocal and unambiguous, forever.

What, then, can be said about polysemy? If it is intended, it enters the intention of the author and the original meaning of the text. And what if it is involuntary or unexpected, brought about by internal relationships within the text? Even if we raise walls, the text may remain open upwards and downwards and over the wall. In the barred garden of the

Song of Songs (4.12) the south wind slips in 'to air the plants and wrest perfume from them'.

When we say that a poem is a self-enclosed entity, we refer to the assembly of its elements in an organic system. Precisely because of this arise numerous relationships that are bearers of a sense which may exceed the calculation or intention of the author.

There is no need to ponder this issue when we pass on to the sphere of symbols, as it is innately multi-faceted and expansive. The author who creates a symbol infuses it with a highly autonomous life, and the entire work may even become a symbol, whether the author thought of it or not.

(4) I end with the multiple and inexhaustable example of the growing of sense of the Old Testament in the light of the New Testament; the illumination of the life of Jesus in the light of glorification. Here, we enter the sphere of faith and the action of the Spirit who, without performing formal miracles, can make use of the proprieties of human language for his own ends.

When Jesus cleared out the temple, 'his disciples remembered what is said in Scripture: My zeal for your house consumes me' (Jn 2.17). This is certainly not what the original Old Testament author thought (Ps. 69.9).

In one of Jesus' controversies, according to John, we read:

> You study the Scriptures expecting to find eternal life in them; it is they that give testimony of me, and you will not come to me that you may have life.
> If you believed Moses you would believe me, for he wrote of me (Jn 5.39, 46).

Writing about one person in particular and the process of giving testimony are two serious and well-defined acts. Must I think that the testimony they gave me about Jesus was a consciously explicit act of the authors of the Old Testament, and that such was their intention in any rigorous sense?

Summary. There are texts with an overflowing richness of meaning: sometimes because the author intended it, or reserved comprehension for a future time, counting on the maturation of the listeners or the development of events. Meaning may transcend the reader's comprehension because of a lack of intelligence or disposition; it may also surpass the author's comprehension.

Chapter 9

THE EXEGETE IN SOCIETY

1. *The Sociology of Knowledge in our Discipline*

Up to now I have spoken of author, text, reader, interpreter, as individuals, as if they were autonomous beings (although plurality has appeared now and again). Now I want to consider them as members of a society.

A literary text is historically conditioned in its production: events, culture, mentality of schools and authors, and so on. We have seen that such conditioning justifies the historical-critical method; but no less conditioned is the reader or receiver of a remote text.

The meaning of a word is defined among other things by the field in which it is found (*langue*), and, by the context in which it is used—sentence and work (*parole*). The comprehension of a text by exegetes is also defined by the context in which they act.

That is to say, the receiver is not usually a solitary person who seeks truth with private means, but a member of a major and minor society, of a political and academic society. In the political society we may also include various economic groupings. Academic society may have a different radius in descending order: the world of science, research and teaching; the university world with its many centres, a specific discipline in the international field; the university and the particular faculty where the exegete works and acts.

We must be conscious of this fact, and hermeneutical reflection will help us to acquire such a consciousness. It would be seriously irresponsible not to be conscious of the effect of social conditions on our exegetic activity. Conditioning is a concept with two facets, positive and negative. It is convenient because it eases or favours work conditions; but it has the disadvantage of limiting our autonomy. In each particular case, both advantages and disadvantages must be weighed, but the fact of conditioning must not be ignored.

The influence of social conditions is far stronger today than, for example, in the nineteenth century. Social conditions powerfully affect our way of understanding and explaining literary texts. The danger lies in the fact that the conditioning factors or institutions sometimes conceal themselves, disguise themselves or slip away.

The *political* factor becomes blatant in totalitarian regimes, a case in point being a biological science dictated by the totalitarian state with coercive power. In democratic regimes, the parties may set themselves up as effective advisers, although with far less force, due to pluralism and the free exchange of loyalties. A particular party sometimes takes possession of, or controls, a particular faculty, denying admittance to whoever does not belong to, or does not submit to the party. Does this also happen in the study of our literary texts, including the Bible? It probably does to a lesser degree.

In our societies, *economic* power is more powerful and active,[1] but it is felt far more in natural science than in the humanities, and, within natural science, it is felt more by applied science or by that with prospective applications. Financing is costly and necessary, and perhaps is accepted by researchers at the price of liberty. Economic power determines at least the selection of programmes and projects of research. The humanities receive secondary attention, which means they are conditioned because they offer fewer jobs and less remuneration. In exchange, the humanities favour pure vocation.

In historical disciplines, including that of the Bible, we must mention the most costly tasks such as archaeological excavations or the publication of works of difficult edition and limited circulation. Libraries often depend on the generosity of businessmen or successful alumni. Since the library is the primary work instrument in our discipline, financial help is converted into a mediate factor of exegetical activity.

Nearer, and more discerning, is the conditioning of the *university* itself in its diverse dimensions. At first, *Universitas* designated the totality of the disciplines to be studied at the mediaeval schools. They were the *universitas studiorum*, and the disciplines were differentiated and hierarchically organized. Hierarchy also reigned among the teachers. Today we may re-interpret the term: the modern university comprises a series of faculties or departments (not all of them), and each teacher belongs to a faculty or department. In addition, the faculty

---

1.　Cf. G. MacRae (ed.), *Scholarly Communication and Publication: Report of the Task Force* (Montana: Council on the Study of Religion, 1972).

belongs to the universal group of parallel faculties. A faculty of Classics or Semitics, of comparitive religions or of the Bible, belongs to an international body of teachers and students who cultivate the same discipline.

Let us try to describe some concrete conditionings with their advantages and disadvantages. If I devote more space to the latter, it is not because they weigh more, but because it is easier to disregard them. Thus, it is not so necessary to draw attention to the advantages.

2. *The Teacher in Society*

Teachers belong to their society, depend on it and are at its service. How do they serve it? By maintaining the *status quo*? As a critical instance? By criticism of both solutions and of ways of stating a problem (which is more radical)? Simply resolving and reacting are two ways of responding to the influence exerted by society.

In the case of secular or religious literary texts, we also belong to an organized society on which we depend and which we serve. Our activity as interpreters is conditioned from above and from below, by the authority we obey and by the community we serve, in questions and answers. Not everything is a neutral investigation of truth. Our activity is conditioned by our ethical conviction or religious confession, and this is probably for the best.

A particular society is made up of the group or body of exegetes or interpreters to which we, in fact, belong. This has brought us an invaluable accumulation of advantages. Other authors, both earlier and present-day ones, have prepared the work instruments for us. Whether I realize it or not, my exegesis depends on the Greek or Hebrew dictionary I use. The plurality of instruments reduces the power of each one, but it does not annul that of the whole. I depend on many work instruments: on the grammar book with which I learned the language, on the encyclopaedia I consult, on my usual or favourite commentaries. My work and my possible contribution are framed before I even start.

The same society shows me the usual work methods, some optional, some compulsory, analysis of literary forms and genres, of tradition and redaction. Why some and not others? Why is genetic reconstruction or the search for sources and influences compulsory, and yet stylistic and poetic analysis unnecessary? Why is analysis of narrative—narratology—suddenly beginning to be important? Why does synchronic study become more important than diachronic study and vice versa?

The interweaving of methods forms a net that both imprisons and sustains us. We move freely in the solutions, but are trapped by the demands of the methods. Woe betide us if we do not follow those who prevail in our discipline! Meanwhile other methods are declared anti-quated and irrecoverable. Is the entire process of methods and method-olgy purely progressional?

The methods we apply also have their own vital curve. They arise or crystallize when an author manages to give them shape and convince others of their aptitude for critical study. Gunkel, who did not invent from scratch, fought, won and bequeathed to us the method of genre criticism. A method is substantiated by its results, it amplifies its sphere of application, it is refined in the hands of a school. There comes a moment when it is exhausted because it has given all it had to give; because it has gone too far and does not know how to keep within cer-tain limits; or because misuse accumulates, making it sterile or perni-cious. Who devotes themselves to finding new literary genres in the psalms? Other times, the method is submitted to revision and produces a variant or something new.

Let us go over some facts. The study of Akkadian, Assyrian, Babylo-nian and Sumerian texts, carried out with great fervour and competence, invaded the territory of biblical exegesis with absolute superiority, bringing torrents of light. It later inclined towards Panbabylonism, which partly discredited the task. A great deal remains of its contribu-tions, and the validity of the comparative study is maintained, but this interest has decreased. For some time, the interest shifted to Mari, Nuzu and finally to Ugarit. Important results were obtained, there were exag-gerations, but new substantial contributions were scarce. What will be-come of the Eblaitic studies, the latest discovery of the ancient Near East? Let us hope it will bring new light.

The study of sources advanced slowly during the last century, until the powerful mind and hand of Wellhausen succeeded in establishing his study on the Pentateuch. The identification and separation of sources went on from the Pentateuch to other biblical bodies, including sapi-ential books. Subdivision was born of the division; new sources were discovered (the N-omadic of Eissfeldt, the L-aical of Fohrer); J and P split into various streams. The method was threatened from within while new techniques lay in wait to supplant it. A fair amount of their contributions remains, although there is no lack of those who deny the existence of a systematic Yahwist or limit the activity to a fraction of the Pentateuch. The study of sources does not dominate our territory today.

Gunkel appeared and, without rejecting outright the study of sources, proposed the study of typical forms that he called literary genres. To each one he assigned its theme, its pattern of development, some exclusive or shared motives, a typical social situation in which it arose or was performed: reciters (rhapsodists) of sagas, cult for the psalms. The contribution of Gunkel and his school has been great and permanent, but today the method seems to have exhausted its capacity for discovery. The universal map of biblical genres is drawn, and there are neither continents nor islands left to be discovered. This method was also misused, with the practice of reductionism that crushed what was individual, and postulated a rigid lineal evolution of each genre. The study of genres is no longer a vanguard position, and does not count with a team of explorers and discoverers.

Some time later came the study of traditions by Alt, Noth and von Rad, three great names in biblical science, each outdoing the other in influence. After this came the analysis of the so-called 'redaction', the study of the genesis of definitive texts by a process of successive sedimentation. This seems to dominate contemporary criticism, although symptoms of fatigue and distrust may be perceived here, too. An opposing front that advances and conquers much ground has been installed with interest in the field of biblical narrative—the study of narrative, with the techniques of 'narratology'. However, the exploitation of poetics to study the extremely rich biblical poetry has not quite asserted itself yet; it has not even established a solid bridgehead.

In these few lines, I do not aim at sketching a synthetic history of the research of the last 100 years. My theme is now sociology, and this rapid survey is intended to show that the exegete lives and acts in a band of critical history. It is a history rich in individual and collective contributions, as well as the inevitable weak points and moments of fatigue. The individual exegete feels carried on or crushed, resists or seeks something new and more effective, but remains subject to a plurality of conditionings.

The themes for doctoral theses are usually suggested by teachers, who tend to consolidate and prolong what they themselves practise. Although the doctoral thesis often makes only a modest contribution, it frequently marks young postgraduates and guides their future work.

Although they may later revise and change their opinions, they will probably not change their approaches or methods.

The teaching staff not only assign themes for theses, but also direct and evaluate them. The teachers' evaluating activity is an accepted bivalent way of conditioning biblical research. It is bivalent because of the tension of the forces that work at a particular moment, which I try to outline below. Tension is a source of dynamism and prevents entropy.

If teachers tend to consolidate a type of study, how can the changes outlined above be explained? It is because two opposing forces work in the academic republic, one conservative and the other innovating.

A certain intolerance of different approaches and methods opposes change. Whoever does not submit will not advance and will not be accepted; a very serious punishment in the academic profession, being a kind of intellectual and spiritual ostracism. But then comes the contrary trend, which is the curiosity to know and to explore new fields. It is a modicum of leaven that is lodged and hidden in the mind of a solitary scholar and makes it ferment; and once it is transformed, the scholar is introduced as new leaven to ferment the larger mass of scholarship. The grain of leaven is sometimes suffocated to death by the enormous mass of the dominant body; but other times, the handful of leaven is more powerful than the mass.

Conservative force is intellectual comfort. One works at ease and with less effort when using familiar instruments. Methods are instruments. Once the professor is firmly installed in a chair, they may get lazy. Their learning and timeworn erudition become the comfortable home of their academic life. On the other hand, weariness acts as a renewing force. We refer to the weariness of what has already been seen and heard; a surfeit of weariness. If comfort can prolong and perpetuate, tiredness is the driving force for change and the impetus in the search for what is new.

To the mentioned comfort, I give the other name of conformism, a most potent conservative force. To a great extent it may be a question of temperament; or perhaps a person is divided into zones: conformist in one field, anticonformist in others. The true opposing force is creative anticonformism. I wish to say that it is not enough to be in disagreement and to undermine so as to demolish what has been established. The important thing is to substitute it for something positive.

Otherwise, conformism will maintain its positions and mock the impotence of the discontent. There are teachers, and not only young ones, who feel the urgency of novelty: to work in virgin ground, experiment with a new method, put new questions, find new approaches to old questions. This is the driving force on the university campus which, being shared, multiplies its creative power.

The student in search of a diploma, the undergraduate in search of a degree, the graduate in search of work, must submit to conformity—in its etymology, the word means to accept the 'form' of another or others—but some in their student stage already feel dissatisfaction and the need for renovation.

Have I drawn away from the theme? I do not think so, because those latent and patent forces condition our comprehension and interpretation of literary texts; and they are forces of social dimension. The academy exerts its influence: immediately, from the teacher on the students of successive academic years; and mediately, on a wider teaching body, through publications.

Summary. Social conditions powerfully affect our manner of understanding and explaining the Bible, political and economic conditions and the university. The exegete lives and acts in a band of that history. The exegete is carried along or resists, conforms or seeks something new and more effective, but the exegete is conditioned. Two opposing forces are active in the university: conservatism and innovation.

3. *To Write, Publish, Read*

a. *Why Write?*

To train oneself: that is, short exercises of method that sometimes contribute to knowledge. To find work: a doctoral thesis, because the university demands a PhD degree. For some, the thesis is the last piece they write and have published in their professorial life (which has its advantages in the biblical field, since it limits bibliographic proliferation). To ascend: an article or book. To ascend is to go up from assistant lecturer to senior lecturer and thence to professor, or to obtain a chair in another, more prestigious, university. To make oneself known: several articles and books, on the same subject, so that the name remains associated with a particular topic and succeeds in being considered as indispensable.

In any valuable zone of a discipline we write to contribute something, to further research, to communicate our knowledge, to confront it with other contributions in a jointly fruitful effort.

> There are sages who are wise for others
> and useless for themselves;
> there are sages who are hateful when they speak,
> and who deprive themselves of exquisite banquets.
> There are sages who are wise for themselves,
> and are laden with the fruit of their knowledge;
> there are sages who are wise for their people,
> and the fruits of whose Wisdom are longlasting.
> He who is wise for himself enjoys pleasures,
> those who see him congratulate him;
> he who is wise for his people inherits glory,
> and his fame lives forever (Ecclus. 37.19-26).

This should be the chief motive, since it cannot be exclusive. In spite of accepting certain conditions, this motive triumphs, simply for the love of truth.

We also write to satisfy publishers of books and periodicals. Book publishers often impose the general theme, according to market forecasts, and so we find the professor trying to be attentive to current consumption. This also has advantages, because publishers may direct the attention of scholars towards present-day problems, at the same time that they offer them a public platform or forum. As regards periodicals, while some suffer a chronic dearth of original articles, others hold back the publishing of an original article for two years. A reasonable limit of publishers' power is that they often allow themselves to be advised by experts in the subject. Such is the case of encyclopaedias and the compound works of several contributors, which show the advantageous aspect of being conditioned.

b. *What Is Written?*
Here I am going to offer a kind of excursus on the discipline it is my lot to practise. The case will probably not enlighten the state of research in other, larger, fields, such as Spanish, English or Italian literature. It may, however, have an analogy with the research of limited areas such as Cervantes, Shakespeare or Dante. The biblical discipline has a special privileged and fateful statute. Privileged, because interest in the Bible has spread among Christians and even reaches some non-Christians. Fateful because the Bible is limited and does not grow.

Spanish literature continues growing; narrative, poetry, theatre and essay. We may study Blas de Otero without stopping at Antonio Machado; a generation of new narrators awaits its dedicated scholars, beyond Cela, Delibes or Torrente Ballester. On the contrary, the Bible is definitely closed, and is not really very extensive, while those who study it increase in number and breed successors. What is to be done?

> If any man adds anything, God will send him the prophetic plagues written in this book. And if any man takes anything away from the prophetic words written in this book, God will deprive him of his part of the tree of life and the holy city described in this book (Rev. 22.19).

Thus ends the last page of the last book of the Bible. How will thousands of exegetes obtain a part of the tree of the Bible? Has its fruit run out?

The first impression is comforting. The Bible has not been exhausted as an area of research. The *Elenchus Biblicus* (the international bibliographical catalogue compiled by Professor R. North) testifies to an abundance of publications, variety of themes and attention to details. If someone consults an article, checking the footnotes, they usually realizes the desire of many to collaborate, to confront oneself with others, to refine one's own work. Pending problems are solved, further knowledge is contributed and points of view are widened. Biblical scholarship progresses at a steady rate.

Since this fact seems unquestionable, we are going to allow ourselves to point out some misgivings with our activity. (I am probably conditioned by my age and by being emeritus.) For instance, it happens that there is a lack of themes for theses, and that theses and articles on the same topic are multiplied in the struggle to arrive first; that each thesis has to devote a long first part to a kind of 'chain' (*catena*) of predecessors, a chain that takes the graduate one or two years to do, and that the contribution made by the new thesis is minute with regard to its bulk.[2]

What is to be done? Why so many theses or articles on the same topic, going round and round like a waterwheel? It happens fairly often that questions without answers are discussed: on the author, the period, the assignation of a verse, on grammar or the lexicon of an incomprehensible text, on a psalm of ambiguous genre. With the facts available to us, the question does not have a probable answer, and so it leaves

---

2. Lain Entralgo recently denounced the same problem, cf. *ABC*, 21 January 1993.

space to guesswork or speculative answers. Thus the following law rules: 'The number of possible hypotheses on a problem is inversely proportional to the number of definite known facts about it'. Questions without answers allow unlimited discussion; and on multiplying the writings on the question, they are given an appearence of seriousness and importance. One more certain fact would suffice to jump from 99 to 100, and the solution would be simple. Discussion would come to an end and with it, a topic for a number of theses. The thesis is important in our present-day academic life. Let us recall the complementary law that says: 'The probability of a hypothesis is inversely proportional to the number of enunciated hypotheses.'

Some scholars object that it is necessary to continue studying for the problem will find a solution. That is an illusion. For the solution to be possible, the known facts must surpass a threshold. Then the scholar will be able to penetrate into the enigma.

It is a different thing to become familiarized with many problems and questions and carry on with our work. It may happen, and it does, that one day we unexpectedly come across the fact that allows us to answer the question under discussion. This is a reply to the misgivings described.

Is there really a lack of topics for biblical research? Is everything said and everything analysed? By no means: there are more than enough topics, but the trouble is that they are not popular. Thus is observed the law that says: 'Populated areas attract population, depopulated ones repel it'. A few discuss the topic, it becomes fashionable, many come along, all of them want to participate in the discussion of the moment. Consult an *Elenchus Biblicus* of 30 years ago in the section referring to Bultmann and his theories: one would imagine that the entire biblical science revolved around his hermeneutical positions.

There is an excess of topics to study. But since only one scholar studies a particular topic, I deduce that it does not interest the academic world and is not worth studying; and that, if I study it, I will be relegated. And I need work, promotion, fame.

How many have studied the world of sentiments in the psalms or in the narratives or in the prophets? Ideas and conceptions are studied, but something as important and difficult as sentiments is neglected and disdained.[3] In fact, social reasons weigh more than the love of truth. It

---

3.   When Bruna Costacurta began her thesis (*La vita minacciata: Il tema della paura nella Biblia Ebraica* [Rome: Pontifical Biblical Institute, 1988]) on fear in

is more important to be known than to know. There we find a powerful conditioning in our task of understanding and interpreting the Bible. Recognition is not the denial of the ample positive aspects of our discipline.

c. *What Is Published?*

A high percentage of the numerous members of the association of interpreters does not write nor publish but depends on what is published by others. What is published? We live in a period of exemplary tolerance but of less exemplary quality. Although filters exist in the editing of periodicals and in publishing houses, the filter has very large holes. If often happens that an article rejected by two magazines is accepted by a third one, because the editor is benevolent, because of commitment to the author, or because the competent editor is absent. There is generous tolerance for pedantry and speculation. We live in a happy realm of civility. The noble side of the medal is respect, no offence, and acceptance; the reverse is permissiveness and mediocrity. Someone will add: a novel insight is not buried thanks to generous tolerance, and will one day be recognized and acclaimed.

Very good and even excellent things are published, but as a whole, quantity has exceeded quality. Publishers have to bring out a minimum number of works a year. If the neighbouring publisher has been successful with a topic, I look for an author to write on the same topic for me. The book business needs new titles, and for those of five or ten years before to become obsolete. The machines cannot remain inert on penalty of not refunding costs. Computers facilitate and accelerate composition. But this is probably more valid for high and medium popularization than for pure research, for which publishers do not contend.

How many complete commentaries on the Psalms are published a year? Ten or twelve. How many articles on the Psalms? More than a hundred. How much is new, not simply said, but truly valuable in the long run? As we forget the preceding decade, the latest work may sound new to us. Ecclesiastes said it, carrying the verdict to the extreme, true to its style:

the Old Testament (fear, not the fear of God, widely studied), she found herself with no biblical bibliography, and had to resort to anthropological studies. She saved herself an enormous amount of reading and wrote an original work, but it was not popular.

There is nothing new under the sun. If someone says: 'Look, this is new' about something, it happened in another period long before us. Nobody remembers the ancients and the same will happen with those to come: their successors will not remember them (Eccl. 1.10-11).

Fathers must be buried to make room for their sons.[4] If a commentator gives priority to the illustrious dead, living colleagues take offence because they are not quoted and followed. It is more important to be known than to know.

d. *What Is Read?*

The volume of what is written and published decisively conditions what is read. Once again I must resort to my personal experience as interpreter of the Old Testament, although it probably applies by analogy to other fields of interpretation. The situation has become very difficult, almost desperate. I can summarize it in a few sentences:

1. There is no time to read all that is written in an extensive field of research;
2. There is no time to read the entire Bible, Old and New Testament;
3. There is no time to read slowly, contemplatively;
4. Lists are read first, and then summaries, so as to choose.

So much is written on, let us say, Isaiah, that I must renounce Jeremiah and other prophets. An expert today is one who knows the entire army of experts in a necessarily restricted field. Thus arises what we ironically call 'the expert in the second act of Hamlet'. The Bible is not known in a broadly unitary cultural context. For example, observe the striking absence of wisdom authors in the studies of other bodies, although the Proverbs provide us with much evidence of a first hand cultural milieu.

Biblical science also lives strongly conditioned by a system of production and consumption and suffers because of it. In a study undertaken 25 years ago, it was proposed that the national or international association should examine the state of the discipline and project its

---

4. In works on Job and the Psalms, many times now José Luis Sicre and Cecilia Carniti have found, in authors of a couple of centuries ago, solutions proposed in good faith as new today (Schultens, Qimchi, Rosenmüller, Ewald, etc).

future along general lines.[5] I may mention that the Spanish Biblical Association planned something similar, and in 25 years has achieved tangible results.

4. *Biblical Exegesis and Society*

This is the most important point, with which we are going to deal briefly. Up to now I have tried to show how the academic society conditions exegetes by favouring and limiting them. Now I am going to take a look at the other society, the people of our time with their problems and desires. What should the interpreter of literary texts do when faced with them? Perhaps the first thing to be done is to distinguish types of text. The ethical question does not appear immediately relevant to Góngora's 'Polifemo', so let us leave a broad space of freedom to poetry. Quevedo and Gracián are different, and to this group the Bible undoubtedly belongs. Let us consider two attitudes: Some shut themselves into their studies and their chairs to follow the discussion of problems that interest exclusively only a select handful of their colleagues. They disregard completely the problems of the time or suppose that personal research will give mediate fruits to solve them. Others open themselves wide, or even more, dive into rough waters to return to their discipline covered with marine salts and filled with the sound of the waves. It is certain that, coming from poverty, oppression and conflict, they will read their texts, the Bible in particular, through different eyes. They will understand it in a different way and explain it in a different key.

Some think that the first type is neutral and is not conditioned, and that the second is conditioned, and dangerously so. Such reasoning reveals a pernicious presupposition: either that many literary texts do not confront the great problems of humanity, or that blindness and deafness are ideal conditions of scientific objectivity.

I am filled with amazement more than once before the blindness of some commentators to see what is in the text: the paradox of God's love and human justice in Isa. 5.1-7, the demands of the disinherited in Psalm 37, the clamour for equality and fraternity in Nehemiah 5. Something fails in that supposed or proclaimed objectivity and neutrality. On the contrary, one who comes physically or mentally from the world of the oppressed heard the clamour of the prophets or the worshippers in

5.   Cf. MacRae (ed.), *Scholarly Communication and Publishing*, p. 160.

the psalms very clearly indeed, while the 'neutrals' lacked receptivity to the big questions of these texts.

What we should not do is bring our answers already formulated to the Bible to find confirmation therein. That would be a new version of the 'argument of Scripture'. Bringing to literary texts questions in search of an answer or of orientation or of inspiration conditions their responses, but neither force nor falsify them. They are conditioned no less by ignoring or eluding the big questions, so as to discuss indefinitely questions without an answer.

The aforesaid must be taken with reserve. As I have affirmed at the beginning of this chapter, the exegete does not work alone, but in a team. It may be that it falls to the lot of an individual to do an apparently neutral piece of work, which allows colleagues to get down to the big questions. The individual's collaboration is thus mediate, but no less effective. That person provides indispensable infrastructure. Although whoever compiles a Greek–Spanish or Latin–Spanish dictionary is not directly concerned with the great problems of our time, they do an immediate service to the group of colleagues and a mediate one to society.

Here I could insert a chapter on 'liberationist exegesis' in its dubious and in its legitimate versions. The distinction of bringing answers or simply questions to the Bible serves as a simplified principle.

Chapter 10

Normative Interpretation

I have explained the correlation between text and society, text and tradition. Without a transmitting society, readers and interpreters, the text
is dead or dormant. An alert text in turn acts on society. The second
correlation is between the text and tradition. However, a society is not
an amorphous mass, but rather an organized and hierarchical body,
within which interpreters have a special place and carry out a specific
function. What Betti calls normative interpretation enters here.[1]

1. *Distinctions*

In order to direct the exposition more clearly, I put forward various
distinctions: for foundation, competence and juridical authority; for origin and use, the inspired, revealed and canonical book; for contents,
belief and conduct; for form, positive and negative interpretation.

a. *First Distinction*

The adjective 'normative' may be taken in a broad sense. A group of
interpreters or an outstanding name establishes standards for their con-
temporaries or those of the future, thanks to their recognized authority
based on competence. I think of Covarrubias (1539–1613) in the *Diccionario de la lengua castellana española*. Recently, Mircea Eliade was
the indisputable authority in the sphere of comparative religions. For all
that, authority, the standard of these interpreters, is not binding; at most
it binds in prudence and modesty. In the era of specialization, competence has acquired a dominating function. Although doctors have no
juridical authority to impose in conscience a treatment or a surgical
operation, prudence advises the acceptance of their decisions.

1.   E. Betti, *L'ermeneutica come metodica generale delle scienze dello spirito*
(Rome: Citta Nuova, 2nd edn, 1990).

Betti takes the adjective 'normative' in the strict sense of a *binding rule,* and presents juridical and religious orders as examples. The Constitutional Court and the Supreme Court may pass sentences that are juridically binding, while experts in law expound or contribute their knowledge. A religious institution may pronounce binding interpretations of their sacred texts: for example, the body of law experts in Islam, the doctors or rabbis in Judaism, the Magisterium of the Catholic Church.

b. *Second Distinction*

Referring to sacred texts, the adjective 'revealed' means that God has communicated it directly to a chosen man or group; 'inspired' means it has been written by individual people moved in some way by God, by God's Spirit (in-spired). 'Canonical' means that it forms part of the official collection of sacred books recognized by the corresponding community. Similar to canonical, but only in the secular sphere, is the concept of 'classical': it is applied to texts that belong to an excellent, exemplary class, and are recognized as such and used. Inspired and canonical are not mutually exclusive, rather they are usually superimposed in the same text.

c. *Third Distinction*

The interpretation of canonical texts may deal with beliefs or standards of conduct. Logically, general or particular standards of conduct usually presuppose beliefs in realities or values that justify them.

d. *Fourth Distinction*

Negative interpretation is categorical and simple: for example, the Constitutional Court of a state declares that such-and-such an action is contrary to the constitution, and so is illegal and invalid. Positive interpretation excludes contradictory or contrary opinion; it does not exclude other possible interpretations.

2. *In Judaism*

We must start from the slow process and final act that determine the 'canon' of sacred books: those which we know today as the Hebrew Bible, divided into the three parts of the Torah (or 'Law'), Prophets and Writings. Judaism does not recognize some of the writings in Greek admitted by the Catholic Church. Within the series, they assign preponderant value to the Law, which they consider to have been communicated by God to Moses and fixed by writing in the Pentateuch. One of the last stages in the establishment of the canon was the synod of Yabne or Yamnia (in the 80s), which follows a middle course between the restrictive tendency of the Samaritans and Sadduceans and the broadening tendency of apocalyptical or arcane writings (Julio Trebolle's detailed exposition, *La Biblia judía y la Biblia cristiana,* should be consulted here[2]).

Among these texts some refer to beliefs, others to conduct. The former (from the *haggadah*) admit and produce multiple interpretations because of the supposed richness of their contents. The latter demand differentiated interpretations to allow for adaptation to the situations and concrete cases that arise. Whose is the responsibility to propose those interpretations with authority?

After the year 70, with the destruction of the temple and the Jewish State, the priesthood disappears. The body of doctors or rabbis, proceeding from the Pharisaic line, survives as the only governing authority. For over a century those doctors devoted themselves to explaining, discussing and transmitting their interpretations of the law (*halakkah*) so as to regulate in detail the conduct of the Jews. At the end of the second century their decisions were codified with binding authority in the Mishnah. Where did this authority come from? Only from a secular human tradition? Or from God?

The doctors resorted to an 'oral Law' revealed to Moses and transmitted by an uninterrupted chain: Moses—Joshua—the Ancients—the Prophets—the Great Assembly. This claim assigns decisive value to tradition and is presented in two versions. The more rigid and difficult to bring into line with the contents of the Mishnah, supposes that Moses received the integral oral Law. The other and more reasonable version supposes that the principles were revealed to Moses, and tradition transmits them as a valid key to interpretation. The doctors possess those keys and apply them with their intelligence, without resorting to personal inspiration from on high. In the chain of transmission, the prophets act as simple doctors, not as legislators. Thus this principle is valid: a doctor (*hakam*) is more than a prophet (*nabi'*): and, taken to the

---

2 .   J. Barrera Trebolle, *La Biblia judía y la Biblia cristiana: Introducción a la historia de la Biblia* (Madrid: Trotta, 2nd edn, 1993).

extreme, prophets and writers will pass away, but the Torah will not pass away.

The contents of the Mishnah bear witness, in many practical questions, to the doctors' diversity of opinions and discussion in the form of dialogue. The definitive solution was reached by consensus or a majority of votes. Once the Mishnah had been fixed in writing with some additions (Tosefta), there followed a stage of new interpretations by the doctors of Babylon (*Amora*). Their decisions were fixed in writing in the Talmud (during the sixth century), which became the standard authority of Jewish Law. From then onwards, interpretations of individual doctors or local or regional rabbinates intervene, but their authority is of simple competence. Not even Maimonides, with his unquestionable permanent authority, proposes normative interpretations.

As a complement, some facts may be observed in the Bible itself. If one examines and compares the codes and laws incorporated into the Pentateuch, a process of adaptation of the laws may be appreciated; it is a literary fiction to attribute all the material to Moses.

On the level of belief, the book of Job bears witness to the three-way discussion between traditional doctors and an anticonformist doctor, with whom the author seems to side. An anonymous prophet (Isa. 56) announces an incorporation of pagans into the people of God, which amounts to the abolishment of traditional laws.

I select two interesting testimonies from two books that are not in the Hebrew Bible. According to Jud. 14.10, Achior, the Ammonite, is circumcised and enters to form part of the Jewish community, contrary to the law of Deut. 23.4. According to 2 Macc. 4.46 and 14.41, two matters as serious as altar stones and the supreme command remain pending a definitive solution 'until a trustworthy prophet arrives'.

3. *In Islam*

In Islam, the situation is neither completely clear nor unitary. First of all, it must be observed that decisions are practically limited to the juridical field, for everything concerning doctrine is considered explicit and concordant. Of the approximately 6200 verses of the Qur'an, some 500 deal with juridical themes.

All Muslim tendencies recognize the Qur'an and the Hadith as binding canonical sources. The Hadith conserves and transmits in continuing and controlling tradition (*isnad*), the Sunna (*Sunnat an-nabij*); that

is, the deeds and sayings of the prophet Mohammed and his companions. The growth of the empire through military expansion, conquests
and the subsequent changes demanded continuing interpretation of the
sources to deduce from them valid applications for new cases as they
appeared. The legislation of Islam is the exegesis of its canonical texts.

Let us begin by proposing some concepts. Who proposes authoritative interpretation? What criteria are followed for interpretation? As
individual persons we may mention the Caliph or legitimate successor
of the Prophet, the local sultan by delegation, the mufti as personal doctor, who solves concrete cases with authority, and the Imam, who
guides the people in prayer and in life according to Islam. Those titles
change in content, and are assigned to different people according to the
times and regions. At first, one single Caliph ruled, and he was the only
Imam. The Ulema, or group of doctors of the law recognized as the
binding authority, acts as a body.

At this point, the two great branches of Islam divide: the Shiite
minority and the Suni majority. The Shiite have a kind of clergy and
hierarchy with authority to decide; at the head is the supreme authority
(*ayatola*). According to a theory that is fairly widespread among Shi-
ites, 12 individuals succeeded Mohammed one after another in the
office of Imam. The last one was abducted to heaven (tenth century),
and will return as a judge to rule the universe (*al-Mahdi*). In his absence, power is exercised by the doctors of the law (*mugtahidun*) with
authority 'to bind and unbind'. Various schools of interpretation arise
among the Suni, but the supreme authority of the Ulema is recognized:
the doctors of the law and religion are the warranters of the Islamic
regime. Consensus is carried out and manifested in them: they correct
and limit, appealing to the law (*sari'a*), the authority of the person in
power, and at the same time, consolidate the state.

The rules deduced from the application of these laws to concrete
cases were then codified. Among the criteria of interpretation, consensus (*igma'*) and analogy (*qiyas*) stand out. Consensus is given when,
after a doctrine has been proposed, no contradiction is manifested
during one generation under a regime of freedom of speech. Analogy
may include the similarity of the cases, deductive reasoning, dilemma,
and so on.

Authority left ample space to schools of interpretation, among which
one (*mu'tazilites*) stood out. This one gave maximum importance to
reason as the interpreter of revelation.

4. *In the Catholic Church*

The Catholic Church has devoted much time to meditating on the present practice of normative interpretation on the part of what is usually called the *Magisterium* (teaching authority). Following the path of reflection, it has arrived at mature formulations. I choose one of these and add a brief commentary to it.

First of all, let us listen to something of what the teaching authority says about herself, in the last solemn authoritative act, the *Dei Verbum* constitution of the second Vatican Council:

> 10b The office of authentically interpreting the word of God.
> The task of giving an authentic interpretation of the Word of God, whether in its written form or in the form of Tradition, has been entrusted to the living teaching office of the Church alone. Its authority in this matter is exercised in the name of Jesus Christ. Yet this Magisterium is not superior to the Word of God, but is its servant. It teaches only what has been handed on to it. At the divine command and with the help of the Holy Spirit, it listens to this devotedly, guards it with dedication and expounds it faithfully.
>
> It is clear, therefore, that, in the supremely wise arangement God, sacred Tradition, sacred Scripture and the Magisterium of the Church are so connected and associated, that one of them cannot stand without the others.
>
> 12d It is the task of exegetes to work, according to these rules, towards a better understanding and explanation of the meaning of sacred Scripture, in order that their research may help the Church to form a firmer judgment...

The first paragraph deals with 'authentic' interpretation (which is not necessarily the technical interpretation practised by philology); done with authority at the service of the word. The formula *vivo Ecclesiae Magisterio* shows that it is an interior body of the Church, and lives in history and tradition. The second paragraph affirms a providential correlation, without explaining in detail of what it consists. The third speaks of the adepts or experts and mentions the 'judgment' of the Church, pronounced by the organ of the *Magisterium*.

Secondly, its description. *Magisterium* can be understood as the teaching activity or as a teaching body. *Magisterium* here means an organ with a function within a community and within a tradition. Its function is to teach and judge or settle, positively or negatively. It exercises its function with charismatic authority.

Said more briefly, the *Magisterium* is an instance in the Church and in tradition, with charismatic authority to expound and decide. 'In the Church', because it is part of the Church and must be understood correlatively. The *Magisterium* is not 'the Church'; it is neither outside nor above the Church. It gathers and guides, expresses and safeguards the faith of the Church. 'In tradition': in the historical movement of faith guided by the Spirit (the tradition described above). The *Magisterium* as a body allows itself to be shaped by the inspired text, and in turn interprets it, on the way to the entire truth. 'With binding authority': if we distinguish competence and authority, we may distinguish a body of people competent in the matter, the 'experts or adepts' who will give their opinion and guide but not impose; and a body with authority to impose and oblige in conscience. That authority is charismatic; in other words, it comes from on high, from the action of the Holy Spirit in the Church, in its members, organs and functions.

In Betti's tripartite division, the *Magisterium* proposes a 'normative interpretation', but it is charismatic, not merely juridical or political as, for example, in a Constitutional Court. It is not that it excludes competence or skill, for it should spare no effort in order to obtain it; but its formal motive of authority is not human knowledge, but rather charisma. Charismatic does not mean miraculous, as if, counting on charisma, human means could be disregarded; that would be tempting God.

'In order to explain and decide': to decide refers to controversial points, and may adopt the form of a trial with a final binding sentence. That sentence may be definitive and unappealable: this is the case of dogmatic definition (conditioned, only, by the language used and the categories in which it is expressed). Even if the sentence is not definitive (ordinary *Magisterium*), and although it is conditioned by the categories of expression, the sentence is binding to a lesser degree, but the *Magisterium* does not always pass sentence in a debate. Most often, it simply teaches authoritatively. The *Magisterium* will also be binding in those cases, in accordance with the type and grade of teaching proposed.

'Positive and negative decisions'. The negative decision excludes a doctrine or an interpretation as irreconcilable with the Church's faith. As a negative judgment, it is unique and exclusive: 'it cannot be interpreted like this'. The positive decision is not inherently exclusive: it proposes a valid interpretation, but it does not so affirm that it is the only one.

Its application to biblical interpretation. As an organ of the Church, the *Magisterium* exercises its function at the service of the community and the text. It is part of the community that reads the Bible and is not above the biblical text. It must therefore guarantee the live presence of the biblical text (reading), and guide comprehension with explanation; in certain cases, it will decide positively or negatively on a particular interpretation.

From the beginning, Protestants have opposed the principle of a teaching authority. However, they recognize the binding and guiding force of the old symbols of faith, of ancient councils and of the profession of faith of the particular group; for example, the '*confessio augustana*' (of Augsburg).

APPENDIX

Three Laws

1. The number of possible hypotheses concerning a problem is inversely proportional to the number of definite known facts about it.

2. The probability of a hypothesis is inversely proportional to the number of enunciated hypotheses.

3. Populated areas attract population. Depopulated areas repel it.

Eighteen Aphorisms

1. The Bible was not written for biblical scholars, nor Don Quixote for Cervantists, nor the Divine Comedy for Danteans.

2. Biblical scholarship is no longer knowledge about the Bible but rather about biblical scholars.

3. More is cooked than is eaten. More is written than is read.

4. One cannot manage to read everything on a theme and feels guilty. One manages to read everything on a theme and feels cheated.

5. Knowing all the data about a text is not yet to understand the text.

6. It is more important to know than to be known.

7. Writing grants the right to be read. Or quoted. Or catalogued.

8. It is folly to utter absurdities; it is erudition to quote them.

9. You will produce fruits with the sweat of your brow: share the fruits, not the sweat.

10. Do not put into the text what the author wanted to leave out.

11. The difficult thing is to hit on the exact question.

12. What was written with imagination must be read with imagination.

13. Follow your intuition; but never confess it.

14. If you do not succeed in explaining it, it is because you have not understood it. If you are obliged to explain it, you will understand it.

15. It is not by being more complicated that the explanation becomes more scientific.

16. Conjecture can be useful and even necessary, but there are problems that fall sick with conjectures.

17. The anti-Ezekiel reduced a living poem to a heap of calcined bones.

18. Clarity is charity for the reader.

BIBLIOGRAPHY

Alonso Schökel, L., *The Inspired Word* (New York: Herder & Herder, 1965).
—*Treinta salmos: Poesía y oración* (Madrid, 1981).
—*Hermenéutica de la palabra*, I (Madrid: Cristiandad, 1986).
—*La palabra inspirada: La Biblia a la luz de la ciencia del lenguaje* (Madrid: Cristiandad, 3rd edn, 1986).
—*Hermenéutica de la palabra*, II (Madrid: Cristiandad, 1987).
—*Antología de poesía bíblica hebrea* (Zaragoza: Delegación de catequesis, 1992).
Alonso Schökel, L., and C. Carniti, *Salmos*, I (Estella: Verbo Divino, 1992).
Alonso Schökel, L., and J.L. Sicre, *Job* (Madrid: Cristiandad, 1983).
Alonso Schökel, L., and E. Zurro, *La traducción bíblica: Lingüística y estilística* (Madrid: Cristiandad, 1977).
Bakhtin, M.M., *The Dialogue Imagination: Four Essays* (Austin, TX: Texas University Press, 1986).
Beauchamp, P., *L'un et l'autre Testament: Essai de lecture* (Paris: Editions du Seuil, 1976).
Bergengruen, W., *Das Geheiminis Verbleist* (Zürich: Arche, 1952).
Betti, E., *L'ermeneutica come metodica generale delle scienze dello spirito* (Rome: Citta Nuova, 2nd edn, 1990).
—*Teoria generale della interpretazione* (Milan: Dott. A. Giuffrè, 1955).
Bleicher, J. (ed.), *Contemporary Hermeneutics as Method: Philosophy and Critique* (London: Routledge & Kegan Paul, 1980).
Bori, P.C., *L'interpretazione infinita: L'ermeneutica cristiana antica e le sue trasformazioni* (Bologna: Il Mulino, 1987).
Coreth, E., *Grundfragen der Hermeneutik: Ein philosophischer Beitrag* (Freiburg: Herder, 1969).
Costacurta, B., *La vita minacciata: Il tema della paura nella Biblia Ebraica* (Rome: Pontifical Biblical Institute, 1988).
Delibes, M., *Cinco horas con Mario* (Barcelona: Ediciones Destino, 1969).
Descalzo, M., *La frontera de Dios* (Barcelona: Planeta, 1956).
Ebeling, G., *Word and Faith* (Philadelphia: Fortress Press, 1963).
Gadamer, H.G., *Truth and Method* (New York: Seabury, 1975).
—*Truth and Method* (London: Sheed & Ward, 2nd edn, 1989).
Girard, M., *Les symboles dans la Bible: Essai de théologie biblique enracinée dans l'expérience humaine universelle* (Paris: Bellarmin-Cerf, 1991).
Graves, R., and R. Patai, *Hebrew Myths: The Book of Genesis* (Garden City, NY: Doubleday, 1964).

Green, J., *Journal* (Paris: Plon, 1961).

Guardini, R., *Die Offenbarung: Ihr Welen und Ihre Formen* (Würzburg: Werkbund, 1940).

Gunkel, H., *Reden und Aufsätze* (Göttingen: Vandenhoeck & Ruprecht, 1913).

Habermas, J., *Communication and the Evolution of Society* (Boston: Beacon Press, 1976).

Hirsch, E.D., Jr, *Validity in Interpretation* (New Haven: Yale University Press, 1967).

Klemm, D.E., *Hermeneutical Inquiry I and II: Classical Articles Selected and Introduced* (Atlanta: Scholars Press, 1986).

Kundera, M., *The Art of the Novel* (New York: Grove Press, 1980).

Ladrière, J., *L'articulation du sens: Discours scientifique et parole de la foi* (Paris: Cerf: 1970).

Lerner, L. *The Truest Poetry: An Essay on the Question: What Is Literature?* (New York: Horizon Press, 1964).

Lurker, M., *Wörterbuch Biblischer Bilder und Symbole* (Munich: Kösel, 1973).

Machado, M., *Poemas* (Madrid: Alianza, 1979).

MacRae, G. (ed.), *Scholarly Communication and Publishing: Report of the Task Force* (Montana: Council on the Study of Religion, 1972).

Madison, G.B., *Hermeneutics of Postmodernity: Figures and Themes* (Bloomington, IN: Indiana University Press, 1988).

Mateos, J., and F. Camacho, *Evangelio, figuras y símbolos* (Córdoba: Almendro, 1989).

Molina, A. Muñoz, *El invierno en Lisboa* (Barcelona: Seix Barral, 1987).

Molina, M., *La interpretación de la escritura en el Espíritu* (Burgos: Aldecoa, 1987).

Moliner, Maria, *Diccionario del uso del español* (Madrid: Gredos, 1966).

Morgan, R., and J. Barton, *Biblical Interpretation* (Oxford; Oxford University Press, 1988).

Mounin, G., *Problèmes théoriques de la traduction* (Paris: Gallimard, 1963).

Palmer, R.E., *Hermeneutics: Interpretation Theory in Schleiermacher, Dilthey, Heidegger and Gadamer* (Evanston, IL: Northwestern University Press, 1969).

Pérez, M., *Los capítulos de Rabí Eliezer* (Valencia: Institución S. Jerónimo, 1984).

Ray, W., *Literary Meaning: From Phenomenology to Deconstruction* (Oxford: Basil Blackwell, 1985).

Ricoeur, P., *The Conflict of Interpretations* (Evanston, IL: Northwestern University Press, 1974).

—*Hermeneutics and the Human Sciences* (Cambridge: Cambridge University Press, 1981).

—*History and Truth* (Evanston, IL: Northwestern University Press, 1965).

—*Interpretation Theory: Discourse and the Surplus of Meaning* (Fort Worth, TX: Christian University Press, 6th edn, 1976).

—*La métaphore vive* (Paris: Seuil, 1969).

—*The Rule of Metaphor* (Toronto: Toronto University Press, 1977).

—*Time and Narrative* (Chicago: Chicago University Press, 1984).

Savoca, G., *Lettura esistenziale della parola di Dio: La nuova ermeneutica biblica* (Naples: Edizioni Dehoniane, 1974).

Ska, J.L., *'Our Fathers Have Told Us': Introduction to the Analysis of Hebrew Narratives* (Analecta Biblica; Rome: Biblical Institute Press, 1990).

Söhngen, G., *Analogie und Metapher* (Munich: Karl Alber, 1962).

Sontag, S. (ed.), *A Barthes Reader* (New York: Hill & Wang, 1982).

Sternberg, M., *The Poetics of Biblical Narrative: Ideological Literature and the Drama of Reading* (Bloomington, IN: Indiana University Press, 1985).

Thomas, J., *Meaning in Interaction* (London: Longmans, Green & Co., 1995).
Trebolle Barrera, J., *La Biblia judía y la Biblia cristiana: Introducción a la historia de la Biblia* (Madrid: Trotta, 2nd edn, 1993).
Updike, J., *Rabbit Angstrom: A Tetralogy* (London: Everyman's Library, 1995).

INDEXES

INDEX OF REFERENCES

OLD TESTAMENT

OTHER ANCIENT REFERENCES

INDEX OF AUTHORS

INDEX OF SUBJECTS